S.O.U.P.S.

S.O.U.P.S.

SEATTLE'S OWN UNDENIABLY PERFECT SOUPS

MICHAEL CONGDON

SASQUATCH BOOKS
SEATTLE

FOR DELIVERANCE

Printed in Canada
Published by Sasquatch Books
Distributed by Publishers Group West
12 11 10 09 08 07 06 05 04   6 5 4 3 2 1

Cover and interior design: Stewart A. Williams
Cover illustration: Bill Quinby/People's Republic of China
Interior Illustrations: Mark Kaufman/Artomat Design

Library of Congress Cataloging-in-Publication Data

Congdon, Michael
        S.O.U.P.S. : Seattle's own undeniably perfect soups / Michael Congdon.
        p. cm.
        ISBN 1-57061-426-1
        1. Soups. I. Title.

TX757.C65 2004
641.8'13—dc22

                                                                        2004046737

Sasquatch Books / 119 South Main Street, Suite 400 / Seattle, WA 98104
(206) 467-4300 / www.sasquatchbooks.com / custserv@sasquatchbooks.com

CONTENTS

LIST OF RECIPES

AUTUMN

I began my journey into the world of soups back in 1994 at a now-defunct restaurant and microbrewery in New Mexico. After a little finessing and much conning I was offered the highly esteemed position of pantry cook at the Rio Bravo Restaurant and Microbrewery. Having already worked as a dishwasher, busboy, barista, bar back, and waiter, I felt I was ready to perform at this level of achievement within the restaurant industry. Of course, with this newly given position, I had to prove my worth in salt. I was promptly placed in charge of making the corn and green chile chowder. This was an item we served daily, so needless to say I made it often.

Eight years, a couple of scars, a couple of burns, three states, and ten restaurants later, I found myself working in an unassuming little place in Seattle known as the Hopvine Pub. It was here, after one of the owners allowed me a very long leash, that I really began to experiment with food. I was able to create many soups, salads, desserts, breads, appetizers, pastas, and dinner specials. Some were successes. Some were silently and ashamedly thrown in the trash. And although I have made many kinds of foods, I always seem to come back to the soups.

People like soup. Soup is comforting. Unfortunately, while many people are comforted and wish to make their own soups, many are also scared of the idea of trying to make a good soup. There are those who can and do. There are those who can, but haven't yet. There are those who haven't and could. There are those who shouldn't and do anyway. And there are those who shouldn't and know better. All of these types, at one point or another, could be found working in the kitchen of the Hopvine.

I could and did—and then I kept going. I figured that by incorporating really good soups and foods into the menu—items a little more unusual or perhaps new and strange to the unwitting customers—I would help draw people into the Hopvine as diners instead of strictly drinkers. When I started, I wanted to make sure I put my thumb so deeply and so securely into the Hopvine "pie" that if I were fired, I would take a large piece of it with me.

Recently while I was watching Emeril on the seductively evil Food Network channel, I began to question my entire purpose for this book. Even though I have learned over the years never to compare myself to others, I still felt a bit of jealousy and resentment while watching this chef make some fancy-schmancy soup entrée. I watched in awe as he prepared this soup using every single appliance in his kitchen setup. When he smiled and introduced this edible objet d'art to all the oohs and the aahs of the studio audience I realized something that transcended the momentary bitterness I was feeling—no one in that audience actually expected to be able to prepare that dish. Those people would just go to Emeril's restaurant and order it off the menu.

Cooks use TV shows and books to promote themselves. That's fine. Unfortunately not many of these cooks are willing to let go of the reins and give the reader/viewer, or simply put, the "student," the knowledge to be able to create the food he or she loves from their restaurant. If the average TV-viewing person watched the same show I had been watching and decided to try to make the food, frustration, aggravation, irritation, stress, anxiety, and angst are just a few of the words that might describe the resulting mood of the individual. This is a shame, because I feel this kind of aggravation and stress is unnecessary and unwarranted. If anything, the general frustration from such an attempt would probably keep most people from ever setting foot in a kitchen again.

This book takes a different approach. Cooking doesn't need to be so complicated. And while I don't believe this book to be perfect, I do believe it will help anyone who wants to learn how to make wonderful, tasty soups.

The Tools section (page 2) is a short list of utensils you might find handy while making stocks and soups. Advice is included about choosing the pieces you invest in, as well as some recommendations for nice-but-not-essential utensils. Actually very little equipment is needed. People who have seen me at work at the Hopvine may have noticed I use only one pot, one big spoon, knives, an oven, and about 6 square feet of prep space—yet I can make these soups. If you have more kitchen resources, you may do even better than I do!

Herbs and Spices (page 4) began as a short list of my favorite spices—then grew! It turns out I have lots of opinions about spices and herbs. Not just which ones go well together but how to bring out their maximum flavor, when to time their addition, even how to locate my beloved Hatch green chilies. With a few exceptions most of the ingredients for the recipes are easy to obtain.

Methods (page 18) describes some basic practices used in many of the recipes. While not overly elaborate, these practices—roasting garlic or making ghee—can mean the difference between "bland" and "complex-with-mysterious-undertones" for your soup. I also offer tips to simplify the preparation and properly handle the volumes of soup.

The chapter entitled Stocks and the Raft (page 27) is the heart of the book. It describes the essence of my approach to soup making. Nothing can really short-cut the need for fresh, seasonal ingredients prepared with care.

After these introductions and preparations, the recipes are presented in seasonal order:

SPRING: Broth with lots of "stuff" in it. Hearty soups that are not rich or heavy.

SUMMER: Cold soups, fruit soups, consommés; thin, simple, and subtle soups. These should complement entrées instead of being the entire meal.

AUTUMN: Puréed soups, thick soups, heavier soups, squash soups, and fish soups. These can have a thin broth, but if so add lots of items to them.

WINTER: Cream soups; rich, heavy, warm, filling soups. Chicken soups, puréed soups, soup-as-a-full-meal soups, fish soups, stews.

One of the most surprising things I experienced with the preparation of this soup book was that during the seeking out of my little "guinea pigs," I decided it would be interesting and wise to have people test the soups—one per person. I was amazed how many people, looking through the recipes to choose one to make, were freaking out about how complicated they appeared. Even my mother, the instigator of my culinary fascination, said my soup recipes scared her.

When I heard these kinds of comments, I recalled flipping through myriad cookbooks while reading the instructions to each recipe. Most cookbooks don't give instructions as explicit as mine. Are the authors of these books trying to write the soup recipes in ten words or less? To me, that type of recipe would be much more daunting had I never made soup before. But because I have, I understand the basic soup construction techniques. This book should provide you with a similar understanding: how to prepare spices, fiddle with ingredients, and, yes, construct a soup!

While the soups in this book are predominantly mine—as in spawned from my own little head—a few are augmentations and alterations of recipes found in various books and articles from my years of recipe reading. This is okay! Having the knowledge to be able to adjust and change what you do or don't like about a recipe is part of the fun, and experimental experience, of making soup. And that is what my book is constantly reinforcing—experimentation.

Experimentation will eventually give a personal signature to your soups. If this signature is a good one then you will be the one people remember when they are planning a potluck. They will call you and say, "Hey! Bring that Carrot, Ginger, and Orange Soup you make so well." Or they will remember your last dinner party and make sure they have enough room to eat a large bowl of your Corn and Green Chile Chowder before you serve your entrée. It really is up to you. Contact me with any questions, issues, suggestions, rants, or raves—professional or personal—at michael@michaelrcongdon.com.

Happy Experimentation!

PREPARATION
AND TECHNIQUES

1

Every craftsman needs tools. While making a soup may not be considered a craft like weaving, knitting, or cobbling, you still need tools. Below is a list of items that are quite handy, and oftentimes necessary, for creating a good-tasting soup. If for some reason you do not own any of them, I suggest you buy some good-quality products. If finances are an issue, then purchase what you can, but do try to avoid the cheaply made.

LARGE SOUP POT: The size of this pot depends on how much soup you plan on making in a batch. I use a 10-quart stockpot because I need a large quantity of soup for the restaurant. For private use, a 4-quart soup pot will be quite adequate.

LARGE SLOTTED WOODEN OR METAL SPOON

SHARP KNIVES: The most common knives I use are a butcher's knife, a 12-inch chef's blade, and a paring knife. Always keep your knives well sharpened. Dull knives are evil! They don't cut well. They can slip from simple things like onion skins and chop off fingers. If you don't have a sharpening stone, take them to a grocery or housewares store and ask if they offer knife sharpening.

FOOD PROCESSOR: Utilize the attachments whenever possible. Do you really want to grate seven large yams? By hand? Do you know how hard it is to purée 6 quarts of soup by hand? Do you really want to mince garlic and ginger? In a word: tedious!

WHISKS: Whisks are our friends.

COLANDER: When straining stock you want a sturdy colander that will not collapse on you, leading to a big splash, many burns, and much swearing.

STRAINER: Cream o' whatever soups and bisques need strainers to reach the proper consistency before serving. Make sure that the strainer is strong and doesn't have any rusty spots on it. Since the mesh can vary, I suggest finding a strainer with a tighter weave since it leads to a smoother soup.

COFFEE GRINDER OR MORTAR AND PESTLE: I use a coffee grinder specifically set aside for grinding spices. A mortar and pestle works fine too. Remember to thoroughly clean out your grinder when you're finished using it. The last thing you want is the flavor of caraway in your Brazilian Black Bean Soup.

CHEESECLOTH: This handy little item isn't used often, but when you need it you will definitely be glad you have it. The cheesecloth usually works quite well in combination with the strainer or colander. I utilize cheesecloth when making *panir* or straining clarified stock.

BUTCHER'S BLOCK OR CUTTING BOARD: Unless you want to scratch and nick your countertop, a cutting board is essential for chopping, slicing, and grating. If all you have is one of those 6- x 10-inch plastic cutting boards that is full when one onion is placed on it (usually it comes as a gift set along with the useless serrated knife from some random dollar store), throw it out and get a worthwhile cutting board.

Remember a couple of rules about using a cutting board. Always set it on top of a towel to keep it from moving around while chopping and always clean it both between items and when finished. Lemon juice or a mild bleach-soaked rag will do the trick here. If the board is wood you don't want to saturate it with water, or it will crack and separate and/or get really porous. If a plastic cutting board still smells like bleach after you have cleaned it, continue to rinse it until the bleach smell washes away. You don't want that odor to lend itself to your soup.

PREPARATION AND TECHNIQUES

STORAGE CONTAINER: This can be anything handy, from a stainless-steel mixing bowl to a plastic 5-gallon bucket. For the soup recipes a 3-quart container will do nicely. It might be used to catch and hold soup going through a strainer, to collect batches of purée from the food processor, or to store the finished soup.

The storage container is meant only to be used as that. Do not reheat the entire batch of soup in it. When reheating the soup, either portion out the amount you want and reheat it the way you prefer, or pour the contents of the container into a pot and reheat it on the stovetop until the soup reaches a temperature of no less than 165°F. Try to avoid boiling the soup. A simmer is perfect.

HERBS and SPICES

Now that you have all your tools laid out before you, let's discuss herbs and spices. They are tricky. You have many variables to remember when using them. Those who grew up in different regions of the country or world have different flavor, aroma, and heat-intensity appreciations.

Unless you have a group of people who are willing to try new and different flavor combinations, it would be wise to try to placate the party. Make a common soup like chicken or potato-leek. Should the group, family, friends, or party be willing to try something new and unusual, flavor the soup to your liking or introduce them to one like Thai Chicken Soup with Papaya and Dumplings, see page 120.

You cannot please all the people all of the time. If you actually try to, you may be giving yourself more frustration than needed. If you are unsure of the party's preferences, I suggest two maxims to follow:

1. MAKE THE SOUP VEGETARIAN. There are also a few vegan recipes floating throughout this book, such as the Tomato Rasam (page 97).

2. FLAVOR TO YOUR PERSONAL LIKING: If a few people don't like it, too bad. You must go with what you know and what you like.

If you are unfamiliar with the flavor of spices and herbs, I suggest you taste them first, in combination, to see if they work well together. If you don't know how strongly they are going to flavor the soup, start off with less and continue to add more until the aroma and taste are to your liking.

While I am on the subject of flavoring, let me briefly discuss salt. Salt can be a thorn in any cook's side. It happens to be one of my biggest pet peeves. If a soup is made properly, there is no reason to add salt at the dinner table. Nothing is more offensive to me than people who ask for salt and pepper before even tasting their food! Unfortunately, people today are brought up on salty food and equate it with flavor. While salt used during the preparing of food does enhance the flavor combinations, salt does nothing when put on a finished dish, aside from making it salty.

That said, I follow a rule when I am making a soup: kosher salt for intensifying, table salt for adjusting. Personally, I use salt when making a soup. When the soup is finished I taste it and decide if the flavor needs to be boosted at all. If so, I adjust the soup to a nice round flavor using salt, pepper, wine, stock, cream, or whatever. Of course the biggest problem about salt would have to be the cook's taste buds. If you know that you have a heavy hand when it comes to salting items for flavor, think before you add or else follow the recipes to the letter. A little trick I have learned in the past is that if you do not keep salt and pepper shakers on the table most people won't want them.

As for the use of herbs and spices, by omitting one you enhance the flavors of the others. By adding one you completely change the flavor combination of all the incorporated spices. Certain spices and herbs mix very well together and others do not. If you are unsure about flavor combinations I suggest following the recipes in the book without altering them—at least until you become more familiar with the flavors of the herbs.

I have to emphasize the importance of using fresh herbs and spices. I am willing to spend a little more money on fresh herbs rather than work with dried ones from a store-bought jar for three main reasons:

FRESHNESS: Quality is much more important than quantity. You simply do not know how long some of those spice jars have been sitting on the store's shelves. Most dried herbs have a six-month shelf life.

COST: If you are going to use dried herbs, such as oregano, rosemary, or thyme, I suggest you purchase only what you need at a whole foods store or someplace where you can buy in bulk. This keeps you from spending money on the jar, the label, and the packaging, not to mention the questionable expiration date. It really is amazing that 4 ounces of thyme purchased in bulk costs you maybe $2 to $3, whereas buying 4 ounces of bottled dried thyme would cost you much more.

FLAVOR: Flavor changes in herbs and spices once they have been dried or roasted and ground. The sweetness of basil becomes nil once dried, and rosemary becomes nothing but sharp little pine needles. (I remember when I was a child my mother had a simple little spice rack that I was always fascinated with. She had a bottle of dried rosemary in the spice rack but never used it. I would occasionally ask her why and her response was, "I don't like its flavor" and "it's too hard to work with." FEH! I knew someday I was going to use rosemary in something and she would like it! I was such a precocious child. I wonder what happened?)

With cumin, fenugreek, or any seeds, as with cloves and cinnamon, it is always better to roast and grind the amount of spice you need, rather than to buy them preground. Roasting brings the aromatic oils to the surface. When ground into a powder the oils immediately begin to dissipate or turn rancid. Therefore the longer you wait to use them, the less intense the flavor.

When roasting spices, just place a small iron or heavy-bottomed skillet on the stove over medium-high heat. Once it is hot enough to cause water to sizzle and evaporate, place the spice in the skillet. Toss it rapidly to make sure all sides get heated through. Watch the spice: You want it to be a couple of shades darker than its original color. ("Ashen" or "black" is not a couple of shades darker.) After the spice has reached a darker color and the aroma begins to waft through the air (in other words, you can really smell the spice), remove it from the skillet and set aside until you are ready to grind it. When I am making soup, I toast and grind all the spices a few minutes before I need them; that way when I am ready, they are ready.

When working with fresh herbs (unless for a stock or something I am going to purée and strain) I remove all the stems and wash the leaves before chopping them. Various herbs like cilantro grow in sandy areas. A quick rinse in cold water is just a good idea.

Before I begin the list of herbs and spices, here are three final topics I want to discuss: chilies vs. peppers, color, and season. These are quite important factors to keep in mind while making any soup—from this book or from somewhere else.

CHILIES VS. PEPPERS: What is the difference? Well, in this particular book there will be some standards I follow when giving recipes and I don't want to confuse the reader. Chilies are the dried and/or roasted pods of the pepper fruit. They have an earthy, slightly fiery, and some-times smoky flavor to them. Examples that I would classify as chilies are Oaxaca chile, chilcos-tle chile, chipotle chile, pasilla negro chile, and ancho chile. There are myriad types of chilies for you to discover and enjoy.

Peppers are the fresh fruit of the pepper plant. They are crisp, juicy, robust, and can vary from sweet and mild to eye-wateringly hot. Examples that I would classify as peppers are green/yellow/orange/red/purple bell pepper, jalapeño pepper, serrano pepper, Thai pepper, and habañero pepper. The term "chile pepper" is both redundant and kind of incorrect in my opinion. Chile equals dried and roasted, and pepper equals fresh. See folks, easy to remember!

COLOR: Color is neither a spice nor an herb, and you are probably wondering what it has to do with anything. Personally, when making bisque or cream soup I feel that colors should be harmonious with each other. Aside from ending up with a murky brown soup, clashing colors can also make something simple like tomato bisque look pale and dull instead of the rich rosy-to-red color it should have. For example, if I am planning to make a tomato bisque I would use red onions and red-skinned shallots for the flavoring. I would also roast the garlic because fire is hot; red is a hot color, so this makes sense to me. I would also use port or red wine instead of white. If I were making a cream of artichoke soup, I would use white onions, leeks, and perhaps fresh garlic. I would use baking potatoes or white flour as the thickener and white wine or cream sherry. Think about what you are using before you use it. Imagine beforehand what color you want the finished product to have. Are the items being incorporated harmonious to that idea or are they not?

SEASON: This too is neither spice nor herb, but something else I feel the need to point out. I try to do a little investigating before I decide which soup to make. What is in season? What is my price range? If you have a lot of money to spend, go ahead and buy out-of-season produce. But be forewarned! Out-of-season produce may not look, taste, or behave the way it would if it were in season. Even though it is the dead of winter and you really want to make an asparagus soup, do you really want to spend the money for lower quality, out-of-season asparagus? Do you want to spend the time looking for it? Better to go with a soup that complements the time of year by using seasonally harvested items. Usually I can tell what is in season because it is either on sale or in large mounds at the grocery store.

Please remember that the descriptions below are how I personally prepare and use spices and herbs. If you have your own methods, feel free to prepare the spices as you normally would.

AJAWAN: Do not let the name scare you. It is actually the seed of the herb oregano. While it does have a hint of oregano to it, the flavor is almost completely different: It is earthy. I really only use it when working with East Indian soups.

ASAFETIDA: This pungent resin, which is related to onion and garlic, is good for two main effects. One is to impart an earthy quality to any Indian dal dish. The other is to help digestion of gaseous lentils. This resin is added after the brown mustard seeds and chopped garlic but before everything else.

BASIL: I use only fresh basil. This herb can turn black and slimy relatively fast so I buy only what I need and use it as quickly as possible. I use the leaves and the flowers, if they exist. I remove the leaves from the stems, then roll them up into a log. I then finely slice the log. Afterwards, I coarsely chop the basil. Dried basil is completely pointless, as one needs so much of it to flavor the soup. The stems are not worth using since there is very little flavor in them. As you might have noticed if you have ever bought herb plants from a nursery, there are numerous different varieties of basil. I suggest if you are unsure about the flavor of each to pick off a small leaf and chew on it. For example, African basil tastes nothing like Thai basil, which tastes nothing like the sweet-leafed basil you buy from the grocer. Find out which best suits you and your dish before purchasing.

BAY: With bay leaves I either leave them whole, if I am using them in a stock, or I crumble them into smaller pieces. Rumor has it that bay laurel is poisonous and that the oracles of Delphi were allowed to chew on one bay laurel leaf a year so that they could experience visions. But when you are using two or three bay leaves in a soup that is going to feed eight

PREPARATION AND TECHNIQUES

to ten people, I don't think you need to worry about any of your guests hallucinating. If you, as the cook, are uncomfortable about using bay, feel free to omit it from the recipes. Bay leaf imparts a nice earthy, woody flavor, but you don't need too much.

BROWN MUSTARD: This spice is left whole. When adding it to a soup, it is important to add this spice before anything else. What I prefer to do is get the oil or ghee in the pot extremely hot and smoking, then add the mustard seeds with one hand and quickly cover the pot with its lid using the other hand. I let the seeds pop for a while. When I no longer hear the seeds popping, I give the pot a good shake. If I still do not hear the seeds popping, I remove the lid and begin adding the rest of the ingredients as needed. When I remove the lid from the pot and I can smell a similar odor to popcorn, I know that the mustard seeds are finished giving their magic.

CARAWAY: I use this in one particular soup. Being that the only spice this soup calls for is caraway, I leave it whole. I prefer people to discover it suddenly. The seed will add its subtle flavor to the soup. The seed itself, however, will still be much more intense. I do not find it necessary to toast this seed. You can if you want to.

CARDAMOM: This spice has two different types to work with: the small green cardamom pods, which are slightly pungent, earthy, and a little intense; or the larger brown cardamom pods, which are less pungent, more earthy, and highly aromatic. If I am feeding people who are not familiar with the brown cardamom pods, they tend to assume these pods are large, dead bugs floating in their soup. You may either leave the pods whole or remove the seeds, toast them, and grind them into a powder. Cardamom is a peppery spice. Both versions work well with coriander, clove, cinnamon, cumin, peppercorn, garlic, and ginger.

CAYENNE: I use this dried and ground pepper when I want to heat up a soup but not really alter the flavor. While a hot spice, it is pretty subtle in its flavoring. Therefore, I use this spice when

I want to keep all the other flavors in the soup up front. The heat will get you, but its flavor won't overpower the soup. I buy in small amounts I can use quickly.

CILANTRO: I remove the stringy stems and wash the leaves. At this point I will either leave them whole or chop them up. This herb should be added to the soup only at its completion or as a garnish. Cilantro is wonderfully refreshing and light, yet slightly spicy. Its flavor can end up lost among the other spices and herbs if added while the soup is being prepared.

CINNAMON: I prefer to break up the cinnamon into smallish pieces and then throw it on the hot skillet to toast for a minute, or until the odor of cinnamon takes over the entire room. Then I either grind it for flavoring soups or I leave it in pieces if adding to a stock. Ground cinnamon works fine also. If I decide to grind my own cinnamon, I sift it a couple of times through a fine-mesh wire strainer. This keeps any large pieces out of the soup.

CLOVES: I don't use many clove buds, but only because not many are needed. Their intensity can overpower an entire soup. Always toast this spice and, again, be careful to watch this process because a clove bud can go from black to ashen in a nanosecond. I grind the toasted buds for most soups, except East Indian dishes where the whole clove comes across just a little bit better. If I do leave the clove bud whole, I warn people before serving the soup.

COCOA: Mexican cocoa powder or any unsweetened cocoa powder works just fine. I blend this with others spices before adding to a soup. Cocoa is great to add to any Mexican dish or soup that requires a form of mole. Just make sure the cocoa you are about to use is not instant hot chocolate—that would be bad.

CORIANDER: As with cumin, coriander seed can be either ground or left whole. I personally like leaving the coriander seed whole. This keeps its earthy and intense, yet slightly fruity, flavor distinct from the rest of the soup. Coriander complements cumin in both East Indian and

PREPARATION and TECHNIQUES

Mexican cuisines. I always toast this spice. When toasting coriander I keep an eye on the pan, as it is easy to burn these flavorful little gems.

CUMIN: I find toasting this seed before grinding adds more flavor to the soup. (Again, watch the pan!) People who like the musky, earthy flavor of cumin will appreciate this added touch. If I want to have an even blend of the flavor throughout the soup, I grind it into a powder. If I want the punchy, earthy flavor or the occasional taste of cumin drifting throughout the soup, I pulse-grind it just to break up the seeds. Leaving the seed whole is fine.

CURRY LEAF: This little leaf has an amazing aromatic kick to it. Usually this herb is used to infuse ghee or oil, which is added at the end of a few of the East Indian soups I have included in the book. This leaf must be fresh when used as it loses much of its flavor as it dries. Most large Asian markets carry this herb in the produce section.

DILL: If I am adding dill to a stock, I toss the bunch in the pot without doing anything to it. If I am using dill to flavor a soup, I remove the leaves from the stems. However, if the stems are very tender I just chop them along with the feathery leaves. Dried dill works fine, but only for flavoring soups, not for adding to a stock.

FENNEL: Use the leaf of this herb like dill, whole or chopped. If I am adding fennel to a stock and want to infuse a great licorice flavor, I leave the leaves on the stem. If flavoring a soup, I chop up the feathery leaves and discard the fibrous stem. I don't use fennel seed too often in my soups, but when I do I like to toast it and grind it up. The nice earthy licorice flavor blends well and people respond to fennel better when they don't actually bite into a whole seed. This seed is also great when making a vegetarian soup. Since fennel seed is the spice often used in sausage, its presence can effectively trick meat-eaters into thinking meat is in the vegetarian soup. This works especially well if incorporating diced portobello, cremini, or white button mushrooms to the soup.

FENUGREEK: An earthy spice, unique in flavor. This spice is golden and very aromatic. Toasting increases its flavor. You do want to grind this spice; it can do damage to the teeth as a whole spice. (Fenugreek leaves are another amazing herb, but the leaves carry a completely different aroma and flavor. So don't use them in place of the seeds!)

GALANGAL ROOT: In the same family as ginger, this tart, citric root can be used fresh or dried. Usually this item can be easily found in any Asian market. Ginger as a substitute in equal amounts will work if galangal is not easily accessible.

GARLIC: Aside from being great for the heart and blood, garlic works well with almost every soup I create. Roasted and puréed or freshly peeled and chopped, it lends an earthy, fiery quality to dishes from all around the world. If I don't want the strong, pungent heat of fresh garlic, I roast it before incorporating. Roasting helps bring the garlic's sugars to the foreground and smoothes it into a very nice mild and slightly sweet flavor.

GINGER: I love ginger. Aside from being a wonderful medicine for the throat, stomach, and blood, I love the tangy, citrus heat it gives. It can overpower, but in the right quantities it lends such an amazing flavor to food. When I am working with ginger, I peel off the skin with the edge of a spoon or a carrot peeler. Once the skin is off, I slice the ginger into ¼-inch-thick medallions to add it to a stock. To add ginger to a soup I will either mince it or grate it. Ginger goes well with many spices but I traditionally use it with garlic, cayenne, cinnamon, clove, cilantro, cumin, coriander, cardamom, brown mustard seed, asafetida, mint, peppercorn, and/ or tamarind.

GREEN CHILIES: Actually a fruit, green chilies have transcended that limited concept and now are used more like an herb. To use green chilies, roast them until the skin blisters, then place in a completely sealed container until the skin loosens from the flesh. Once the skin is loose, gently peel it away. Then remove the stem and the seeds. Chop up the chile and you are ready to go.

I suggest you avoid using canned green chilies as they are extremely expensive and very bland compared to the frozen variety. I am loyal to chilies from Hatch, New Mexico. The flavors of Hatch green chilies range from mild to very hot. Sadly, they are pretty hard to locate outside of the deep Southwest (that is, New Mexico and Arizona). But do not despair. Folks outside the southwestern U.S. have two ways to acquire Hatch green chilies. The first is through the Internet, the second is if you know anyone in New Mexico or Arizona who can mail them to you. These chilies are worth it.

GROUND RED CHILE POWDER: I purchase this ground spice in bulk when I need it. I use it for Mexican soups if I want flavor and a spicy touch. Its heat varies depending on whether I purchase mild or hot chile powder. It lends a great flavor that combines well with cumin, coriander, clove, cinnamon, cocoa, and garlic. Do not confuse with chile powder, which is a blend of spices to flavor chile and chile con carne stews.

LIME LEAF: Kaffir lime leaf is exactly that, the leaf of a lime tree; it can be easily found at Asian markets. Nothing can really substitute for its flavoring. If you can't find lime leaf, simply omit it from a recipe.

MARJORAM [WILD OREGANO]: Lots of people avoid this herb because they don't really know much about it. When working with marjoram, I remove the leaves from the stems and give them a coarse chop. If I am making a stock, I will leave the stalk whole and add both the leaves and the stalks to the stockpot. Dried marjoram is quite bland and not really worth using. Marjoram blends well with savory, thyme, oregano, and rosemary.

MINT: Use only the fresh herb. I remove the leaves from the stems and wash them gently. Sand can easily get trapped in the coarse and textured leaves. I roll the leaves up as I do basil and finely slice it. With its strong flavor, I prefer to only use mint as a garnish for my soups.

NUTMEG: This spice can overpower a soup, but it takes way more than you would expect to achieve this effect. I prefer to buy whole nutmeg and grate it as needed, resorting to preground nutmeg only if I have no other options. Once you smell the aroma of freshly ground nutmeg you will understand why. I am not shy about flavoring with nutmeg since most of the soups to which I add nutmeg have very few, if any, other spices added and tend to be very subtle in flavor. Nutmeg works well with cinnamon, ginger, clove, cardamom, allspice, and black pepper. Its flavor is exotic, peppery, kind of hot, and generally spicy.

OREGANO: I prefer to remove the leaves from the stems and coarsely chop them. If there are flowers on the tips of the stems, then lucky me! The flowers tend to be much more pungent and peppery and can really add a punch to the seasoning of a soup. The stems have some flavor, but not enough to really bother with. I will also use the dried herb if that is all I have. Dried oregano has a flavor similar to the fresh—though a little more earthy and a little less peppery.

PARSLEY: I always seem to use the curly parsley. If you prefer, you may use the Italian variety whose leaves are larger and flat. With both kinds, leave the parsley whole if adding to a stock or remove the stems and finely chop the leaves up. I like to add parsley just as I'm finishing the soup, either into the soup with the last stirrings or floating on top as a garnish. Parsley is one of those herbs with a subtle and green flavor, which works well with just about every western herb.

PEPPERCORNS: This spice is best used whole or slightly cracked when flavoring soups or stocks. If you want to heighten the aroma and peppery flavor, try roasting them before cracking. This gives a little more heat and intensity to the subtle fire within. Pepper has the ability to become slightly musty and taste like hot granules of nothingness if bought preground and allowed to sit for a long time on the shelf. Again I urge you to stick only with whole peppercorns and only grind the amount you will need at the time. As a whole spice, its shelf life is extended greatly. Try to remember this little list for your future usage of peppercorn:

Whole if flavoring a stock.

Whole or cracked if adding to a soup that will be puréed and strained.

Cracked or ground if added to a soup for flavoring.

Ground when adjusting flavor.

ROSEMARY: If I am flavoring a stock, I leave the rosemary as a branch and throw the whole thing into the stockpot. The branch itself, while very woody and tough, does contain a lot of flavor so don't discard it. When flavoring a soup, however, remove the leaves from the stem and give them a coarse chop. I do not use dried rosemary unless I want sharp and bland needles in my soups—which is never.

SAFFRON: This wonderful herb can be overpowering if not used correctly: ¼ teaspoon of saffron is enough for 10 quarts of soup! The best way to work with this herb is to soak a pinch in hot water or hot milk. Use your saffron. After six months, both the flavor and color lose their intensity. Store saffron in a cool, dark place. Sunlight will ruin it.

There are many inferior-quality so-called saffron producers out there. Sadly, the only way I know to make sure I get real saffron is to spend a lot of money for a very small amount. It should have a flowery yet exotic aroma about it. Should these little reddish-golden stigmas smell like marigolds, you have been ripped off. They will neither correctly color nor correctly flavor the soup.

SAGE: Sage comes in many different varieties, colors, shapes, and sizes. I prefer to use rubbed sage, which I can purchase in bulk, or fresh sage. If I am using fresh sage, I remove the stems and roll the leaves together, thinly slice the leaves, then give them a coarse chop. If I am planning to add the sage to a stock, I just remove the leaves from the stems and toss them, whole, into the stockpot. If I don't particularly want the somewhat musty, dry flavor some of the more common varieties of sage offer, I will use pineapple sage. This variety, in particular, offers a bit of a lemony, pineapple-ish exotic flavor to the soup.

SAVORY: This herb has a flowery, wonderful aroma. I prefer to remove the stems and chop up the leaves and flowers. If I am adding this herb to a stock, I leave the stems intact and toss the whole herb into the stockpot. I wouldn't even think of using this herb dried.

TARRAGON: Related to wormwood, this subtle licorice-flavored herb is great for infusing white wine or champagne vinegar. When using tarragon I either chop up the whole herb or remove the stems and give the leaves a few chops with the knife. The mild flavor of tarragon works well with fennel and anise. Be careful when blending it with marjoram, thyme, oregano, and/or savory herbs as its flavor can easily become muddled.

THYME: I like to remove the leaves from the stems, an easy process if the stems are sturdy and thick. If the stems are young and just as tender as the leaves themselves, I chop up the whole herb, using stems, leaves, and flowers, if present. It is one of the few herbs that maintains its flavor once dried, and I use the dried herb when I have no alternative.

PREPARATION AND TECHNIQUES

I always tell people that making soup is not a one-step process. One doesn't just throw things into a pot, turn on the heat, and call it done. Making soup takes some time, some effort, and some preparation. One of the things I like to do is change the composition, or flavor, of items before adding them to the soup pot. This section will give you a brief overview of how to roast garlic bulbs, roast eggplant, roast squashes, or bake potatoes—just in case you don't already know. If you find this chapter to be a little too basic for you, skip ahead and jump into the soup recipes!

APPLES AND PEARS: So you found a recipe calling for apples or pears. Unless the recipe calls for a specific variety of apple or pear, go with whichever you personally like. You will never see me chomping down on a Granny Smith apple. I don't like Granny Smith apples raw. However, I do occasionally use them in my soups when their flavor blends well with the other ingredients I am using.

Soups with apples and pears tend to be made in the fall and winter when they are most prolific. Your grocer will have many different varieties of apples and pears mounded all over the place—so which type should you buy? Well, I guess it really depends on what you plan on doing with the apples or the pears. All the recipes in this book will need the pear sliced so you will want to use crisp, sweet, and ripe pears. Ask your grocer or look around for pears that remain crisp and juicy when they are ripe. If you are dicing the apples into small cubes, you are going to want a nice crisp apple that will hold its shape when being sautéed and boiled. If you are planning to purée the apples, I suggest a more coarse-grained type, a mealy apple. So experiment! Taste each different type of apple and pear and see which ones you prefer. If you know what you prefer, work with your personal favorite. If you want to use Granny Smith apples in your Beet and Apple Soup with Sour Cream and Fresh Dill (page 146) then by all means, do so! When making soup, I prefer to use Fuji, Cameo, Mutsu, Braeburn, and, yes, even Granny Smith apples.

BEANS AND LENTILS: Some of the recipes call for canned beans and some call for dried beans— for a reason. Some dried beans have to soak for a really long time. Mooth lentils need at least 12 hours of soaking before they can be used. Garbanzo beans require at least 8 hours. Black beans can be soaked up to 24 hours before being used, but black beans can also be cooked without presoaking them. Lentils need to be soaked for 2 hours before using them. If you don't have the time to do this soaking and you need to make a quick soup, canned beans work great in a pinch. When buying the canned version of these beans, make sure they are packed in water and there are minimal or no spices added to them. If you are using lentils, I insist you soak them, since canned lentils are not available to my knowledge.

EGGPLANT: When working with eggplant, I roast it just like squash. However, the eggplant will take 45 minutes to roast. Once roasted, I let it cool for about 20 minutes. When cool enough to handle, I wedge my fingers just below the skin and pull it away from the meat. I purée the skinned eggplant and then press it through a strainer. This separates the meat from the bitter seeds. At this point you are ready to use it as a soup base.

GARLIC: Perhaps I want to roast my garlic before adding it to the soup. This is an easy task. I preheat the oven to about 450°F. I take however many heads of garlic I need and slice the tops off them. I set the garlic heads in a small pie tin, face up, with the raw cut cloves exposed, and add 2 tablespoons of water per head in the pie tin. I place ½ tablespoon of butter and drizzle ½ tablespoon of olive oil over each head, then cover the entire pie tin with aluminum foil. I want to make sure the seal of the foil is tight because I want the steam from the water and butter to keep the cloves of garlic moist. I set the pie tin in the oven and allow the garlic to bake for about 45 minutes. When I think it is finished, I remove the tin from the oven and carefully pull off the aluminum foil. I take a paring knife and try to insert it in the cloves. If the knife slides in, then the garlic is done. If the cloves still feel like they have a texture other than mushy, back into the oven they go for another 10 minutes—at which point I test them again. I repeat this process until the garlic reaches the proper consistency. So now I have roasted or baked garlic.

Once they have cooled off, I take the garlic heads between my fingers and gently squeeze out all of the cloves from their skins. I can, at this point, store them as whole cloves or purée them into a paste.

GHEE: Ghee is simply clarified butter. When making ghee, I make a large amount because it lasts a long time and its preparation can be time-consuming. First I place 1 pound of unsalted butter in a small pot, turn the heat to medium, and let the butter melt. When the butter has turned to liquid, I let it boil for about 20 minutes. While the butter is boiling, I place three or four layers of cheesecloth in a strainer, then watch the butter to make sure that it doesn't burn. Once the bubbling has subsided and the crust on top has turned a golden color, I remove the pot from the heat and quickly strain the clarified butter through the cheesecloth, discarding all the dark-brown and black lumps remaining in the strainer. I now have clarified butter.

Clarified butter is, in essence, butter oil—it no longer has any milk solids. The best part about ghee is it cannot turn rancid. The milk solids, which have been removed, are the particles that lead to butter going bad. A very soft solid at room temperature, ghee has a nutty flavor unlike regular butter. Purchase it at the grocery store to save time, but feel free to experiment and make your own.

OILS: Many different types of oil exist in the world—walnut, olive, sesame, canola, corn, safflower, avocado, coconut, peanut, ad nauseam. Which ones should you use? It really depends on the ethnicity of the soup you are making. Indian, Thai, Chinese, and Japanese soups and dishes never call for olive oil. Stick to the region is my personal philosophy. Coconut, avocado, or a simple canola oil, or ghee, work fine for Indian soups. Sesame, peanut, soy, or canola oil work perfectly for Chinese, Japanese, or Thai soups. Olive oil works well with most other regional soups. Finally, butter is perfect for bisques and chowders.

POTATOES, SWEET POTATOES, AND YAMS: There are five classic ways to thicken a soup: flour, rice, potatoes, nuts, or reduction. Since I prefer to add a starch I would immediately forego both the reduction and the addition of nuts to the soup. If the soup is delicately flavored, I would also omit the addition of flour, which can leave a somewhat pasty flavor. Rice also does a good job as a thickening agent; however, if I am not watching over my soup constantly, the rice can quickly burn to the bottom of the pot and add a scorched flavor to the soup. Personally, I usually stick with potatoes.

When dealing with potatoes, I prefer to bake them. I heat the oven to 550°F, place three or four scrubbed potatoes inside and let them bake for at least an hour. I want to make sure the potatoes are completely cooked, so after an hour I test doneness by inserting a sharp knife. If it easily slides all the way through, the potatoes are done. If they seem to have a little resistance, bake the potatoes for another 15 minutes and test them again. This all depends on the size of the potatoes—larger potatoes take longer to bake.

What next? I take the potatoes out of the oven and slice them in half. I get my food processor set up, grab an oven mitt and a spoon, and proceed to scrape all the potato flesh into the food processor. When I am left with the crusty burnt skins of the potatoes, I toss them out and turn on the processor. As the steamy, hot potatoes are being puréed, I add a little stock to them, which helps the potatoes thicken into a pasty substance. This is a good thing! Once the texture is smooth and has no obvious lumps, I remove as much potato from the processor as possible and set it aside to use at the right time.

PREPARATION AND TECHNIQUES

When I am making a creamy yam soup, I place an appropriate number of yams or sweet potatoes in the oven and bake them for roughly 1 hour, or until they are quite soft—I test their doneness the same as I would regular potatoes. At this point I remove them from the oven and let them cool enough to handle easily. Peeling roasted yams and sweet potatoes is easy as long as they are still warm enough and the skin hasn't begun to stick to the flesh inside. I purée yams and sweet potatoes in the same fashion I would regular potatoes. I prefer garnet yams. They are not too expensive, have a lovely red color and a wonderful sweet flavor that really surfaces with roasting.

SQUASH: While pumpkin makes a great soup, so do many other gourds and squashes. And if you want to spend quite a bit of time peeling and cubing a butternut squash, go right ahead. However, other—easier—methods add a different dimension to the flavor of the soup.

Say I want to make an acorn squash soup (and this works well with every other squash), I slice the acorn squash in half and scrape out the seeds. This done, I set my oven to roughly 500°F, grab a clean jelly-roll pan (or something with a lip to it, so none of the squash's water runs out onto the heating element) and brush a light coating of vegetable oil on it. Next I take kosher salt and coat a flat dish with it. I take the squash, place it cut side down, press it into the salt so the salt adheres to the flesh, then tap the squash lightly to remove any excess salt. Then I set the squash, cut side down again, onto the pan and place it in the oven for at least 30 minutes. Some squash will take longer, a few of them will take shorter, amounts of time to cook. Normally, unless the gourd has a very stiff and thick skin, I can tell when the squash is done because the skin is loose and the flesh falls away easily. After the squash is finished cooking, I remove it from the oven and let it cool until it is easy to handle. At this point I scrape the meat away from the skin and place it into my food processor. I purée this, with a little vegetable stock, into a nice, smooth, velvety, thick stock. This should have a consistency similar to canned pumpkin purée.

TOMATOES: I have some fresh red tomatoes. How do I get the skin off and the seeds out of them? First, I get a large pot of water boiling and fill a large bowl with ice and cold water. While heating the water, I make little **X**s on the bottoms of the tomatoes with a paring knife. Once the water boils, I add a few tomatoes at a time, wait about 1 minute, then remove the tomatoes and place them directly into the ice bath. As soon as I see the skin pulling away from the **X**s, I peel off the remaining skin. Then I slice the tomato in half horizontally, stick my fingers into the little pockets and easily slide the seeds and juice out of them. Saving the juice from the tomato is a good idea. I use a strainer set over a bowl. I remove the seeds over the strainer and let the juice drip from the tomato's cavity, down my hands, through the strainer's metal mesh and into the bowl. This leaves me holding the flesh, which is ready to be chopped up and added to the soup.

Again, these suggestions are simply that, suggestions. You can follow them or not. It's not as if I will be standing behind you while you are making your soup, slapping your hands when you are doing something wrong. I may be outside lurking and staring through your kitchen window, but certainly not behind you . . . .

Finally, a few tips to make creating soup much easier and more exciting:

1. Get everything ready before you start mixing, combining, or cooking. This is the only way you will know you definitely have everything you need.
2. Nothing makes me yawn more than seeing everything in the soup the exact same size. If I am making a minestrone soup, or a soup with a lot of vibrant colors, I try to vary the sizes and cuts of the freshest and brightest of various fruits and vegetables so each has its own distinct look.
3. Roasting adds more flavor than boiling.

If you are making a soup from this book and you just know in your heart of hearts that something else added would make it better, by all means do it. Just remember to think about what you are adding and when would be the appropriate time to add it.

PREPARATION AND TECHNIQUES

Soup is in fact a very simple thing to make. What is difficult is figuring out when the various ingredients should be joined together. Soup is not about throwing all of the ingredients into a pot, adding water, and calling it dinner. Soup is about time and flavors that need this time to be melded into a harmonious flavor spectrum. I could say, "This tastes like onions" or I could say, "Mmm . . . yummy, yummy, yummy!" If everything is thrown in together at the same time, the specific flavors remain separated. This can be a bad thing and is probably the biggest problem I have experienced with soup making. If I am hurried, I know the final result will be under par. Let each ingredient work its specific magic before adding the next.

Think about what is in season. When you are in the grocery store, look around the produce section. What items do they have vast quantities of? What items are on sale at ridiculously cheap prices? These items are most likely in season and are ready to be used. Would you buy fresh strawberries in November? No. They are not only more expensive, but likely to be of inferior quality to those purchased in late spring and early summer. This goes along with the idea of maximizing the flavor of your food. If you buy vegetables and fruit not naturally ripened or in season, their flavors are going to pale greatly next to those that are.

Each recipe is written assuming you will be serving the soups promptly. If you are preparing soup for the next day or you are planning on making a large quantity of soup (or stock) to eat over the course of a couple of weeks or months, use one of the following techniques for proper cooling.

The key is speed: You want to get the soup from "too hot to grow bacteria" to "too cold to grow bacteria" quickly. Pour the soup into a wide shallow pan and slide the pan into the refrigerator. Or pour the soup into a sturdy plastic container, and either stir the soup rapidly over an ice bath until it is cool to the touch, then place the covered soup container in the refrigerator until you are ready to consume it; or fill an empty 20-fluid-ounce soda container with water, freeze it, submerge it in the hot finished soup, then place it all in the refrigerator, uncovered.

Both of these methods will quickly cool down the soup. Do *not* cover the soup while still hot. The trapped heat inside the container will condense from the colder outside air leading to bacterial growth, which can cause food poisoning.

Homemade soup has a refrigerator shelf life of about 1 to 2 weeks. If you are planning to store the soup for a longer time, I suggest either canning the soup in mason jars while still hot or chilling the soup in the refrigerator and then freezing it in freezer-strength plastic bags. If you do decide to can the soup, follow the instructions in your canning manual. Freezing will work for most of the soups; however, with cream-based soups you will need to add the cream only after thawing the soup while you are reheating it. (In other words—don't freeze the cream.) I will also warn you that freezing certain vegetables can lead to discoloration and an overall texture change of the soup. So a once-vibrant green soup may end up with a dull khaki or a light brown discoloration. If you are planning to produce a large quantity of stock, may I suggest you store the stock in 2- to 4-cup containers, enabling you to thaw only what you need.

I know quite a few people who are morally offended or shocked and disturbed by the occasional use of a microwave to quickly heat up a soup. My maxim is: whatever works for you. If you use a microwave, I suggest adding a couple of tablespoons of water to the soup so it doesn't thicken too much. If you use a stovetop I suggest reheating the soup over medium to medium-low heat until it just begins to simmer, stirring occasionally so you don't scorch or burn the soup. Soup should never be reheated to a boil. If you plan on reheating the soup and keeping it warm for a while, you must keep it above the minimum temperature of 165°F. If you keep the soup between the temperatures of 40°F and 140°F, your soup becomes a veritable playground for bacteria. This does not include canned or properly jarred soups, only those open and exposed to air.

Remember, nothing says love like a belly full of soup. If you put good energy into your soup, people will know it and admire your fabulousness.

PREPARATION and TECHNIQUES

STOCKS AND THE RAFT

Because this is a simple soup cookbook, I am avoiding going into detail about various types of lamb or veal stock. For our purposes, stocks can be either vegetable, fish, chicken, or even just water. This is really up to you.

To make a good chicken stock you need to be willing to let the pot simmer for up to 10 hours. I suggest starting it at night and finishing it in the morning. The only question is "Are you willing to ignore the stovetop all night even though it is actually on?" This is your call. If you want to make a homemade stock and are not willing to sleep or ignore the stovetop, then you have to be willing to spend quite a bit of time in front of the stove doing nothing, or talking on the phone, or working a couple of crossword puzzles, or watching *The Bad Seed* 3.6 times—Rhoda was simply a darling. Do what you want.

This makes a lovely light fish stock. You will notice that compared to the vegetable and chicken stocks, I use very little in the way of strongly flavored veggies. With this stock, it is important to allow the flavor of the fish to stand out.

>   5 quarts cold water
>   2 yellow onions, chopped with skins still on
>   2 ribs celery, washed and chopped
>   2 shallots, chopped with skins still on
>   1 carrot, washed and chopped
>   1 bulb fennel, washed and chopped
>   ¼ cup kosher salt
>   6 pounds of fish, no skins or scales (I prefer cod or salmon)
>   2 cups white wine
>   1 bunch dill
>   1 bunch parsley
>   8 bay leaves
>   2 tablespoons black peppercorns

1. Assemble a 10-quart stockpot, a colander or strainer, cheesecloth, and a 6- to 8-quart storage container. Get out your spoons and knives.

2. Place the water, all the vegetables, and salt in your pot, cover and set it over high heat.

When the water begins to boil, lower the temperature to medium. Keep the pot covered and simmer for roughly 1 hour, or until the vegetables begin to fall apart. Pour the liquid into a strainer that had been placed over a container large enough to hold all of the liquid. Let the vegetables drain for a few minutes then discard them, reserving the liquid.

3. Place the fish into the soup pot along with the wine, herbs, and peppercorns. Pour the reserved liquid back into the pot. Cover the pot and set it back onto the range over high heat. When this liquid begins to boil again, lower the heat to medium and allow the stock to simmer for a minimum of 2 hours.

4. Carefully remove the fish pieces from the stock and discard them. Then pour the stock through your strainer into your storage container. Discard all the bits and parts left in the strainer and set the stock in the fridge to cool. Remember: Don't put a cover on the hot stock. Otherwise it can turn bad very quickly. Once the stock has cooled sufficiently, you can store it until further notice, use it immediately, or clarify it with a raft (page 37). When making a raft for the fish stock, do not use carrots—just increase the amount of the celery and onion.

This basic vegetable stock has a great flavor that you can personalize by adjusting the herbs and vegetable quantities. But whatever you do, avoid adding tomatoes, eggplant, zucchini, squashes, or any peppers; these vegetables can cause the stock to become extremely bitter.

2 to 3 yellow onions (skins left on), washed and quartered
2 shallots (skins left on), washed and quartered
2 medium-large leeks, including green parts, washed and roughly chopped
2 heads garlic (skins left on), washed and broken up
6 to 8 bay leaves
1 bunch oregano, including stems, washed
1 bunch parsley, including stems, washed
1 bunch thyme, including stems, washed
2 tablespoons kosher salt
1 tablespoon black peppercorns
2 cups dry white wine
3 carrots, washed
1 bunch celery, washed, leaves, heart, and bottom included
1 parsnip, washed and quartered
1 turnip, washed and quartered

1. Assemble a 10-quart stockpot, a colander or strainer, cheesecloth, and a 6- to 8-quart storage container. Get out your spoons and knives.

2. Place the onions, shallots, leeks, and garlic with 2 cups of cold water in the stockpot. Cover the pot and place over high heat until the water begins to boil. Reduce the heat to medium and simmer for 15 minutes, or until the vegetables become soft.

3. Add the herbs, salt, peppercorns, and wine to the pot. Stir well. If the water has started to evaporate, add another 2 cups. Cover and let simmer over medium heat for another 15 minutes.

4. Add the rest of the vegetables and fill the pot with the water to 2 inches from the rim. Cover and allow the liquid to reach a boil. Once the water is boiling, reduce the heat to medium-low, keep partially covered, and allow to simmer for 2 to 2½ hours.

5. Once the liquid has turned a lovely dark brown color, remove it from the heat and strain through a colander into the storage container. Allow the contents of the pot to drain for a few minutes before you discard the remains from the colander.

6. Clean the soup pot and place a strainer lined with cheesecloth over it. Slowly pour the stock through the cheesecloth, stopping occasionally to help the blocked stock get through the cheesecloth. Now the stock is finished.

7. You can use the stock now or cool it in an ice bath, whisking until it cools sufficiently for storage in the refrigerator. Alternatively, freeze the stock in smaller portions or jar it following the instructions of your canning manual.

S.O.U.P.S.

I've had quite a few compliments on this chicken stock. For added pizzazz, include a ½ teaspoon of saffron threads when adding the chicken to the stock. If, after running the stock through the cheesecloth, it still tastes bitter, I suggest adding a cup of sweet white wine to it.

3 carrots, washed
1 bunch celery, washed, leaves, heart, and bottom included
2 heads garlic (skins left on), washed and broken up
2 leeks, including green part, washed and roughly chopped
2 to 3 yellow onions (skins left on), washed and quartered
1 parsnip, washed and quartered
2 shallots (skins left on), washed and quartered
1 turnip, washed and quartered
2 tablespoons kosher salt
2 whole chickens
6 to 8 bay leaves
1 bunch dill, including stems, washed
1 bunch parsley, including stems, washed
1 tablespoon black peppercorns
2 cups dry white wine

1. Assemble a 10-quart stockpot, a colander or strainer, and a 6- to 8-quart storage container. Get out your spoons and knives.

2. Pour about 1 quart of cold water into the stockpot. Set the pot over high heat. Coarsely chop all the cleaned vegetables, skins and all, and place them in the pot with the cold water. Cover the pot and let the water reach a boil. Reduce the heat to medium and simmer for about 30 minutes, or until the vegetables begin to soften. Add the salt and stir well. Fill the stockpot to 1 inch from the top with cold water. Cover and return to high heat. Once the water starts to boil again, lower the heat to medium and allow the stock to simmer for roughly 2 hours.

3. While the stock is simmering, chop the chickens, including the bones, into 3-inch pieces, reserving the breast meat for the soup. Discard or use the skin, as you wish. Place the chopped-up chicken pieces in a container and refrigerate until you are ready for them.

4. After 2 hours the stock should be golden in color and the vegetables should be falling apart. Taste it: Don't worry if it tastes slightly bitter. The wine, herbs, and chicken will take care of the natural bitterness of the vegetables.

5. Remove the stockpot from the heat and strain the contents through a colander into the storage container, allowing it to drain for a few minutes. Occasionally shake the colander to help free any trapped liquid. Once all of the liquid has strained through, discard all the mushy vegetables. You don't need to clean the pot as everything is going right back into it.

6. Place the storage container in an ice bath. Stir the stock with a whisk until it cools to below room temperature. This should take 2 to 3 minutes. The chicken should be added to cold water.

7. Place your raw, chopped-up chicken parts in the empty stockpot. Add the bay leaves, dill, parsley, peppercorns and wine. Return the stock to the pot. If you can't put all of the stock in the pot, just remove some of the water until you can fit all of the chicken parts in the pot. However, you'll probably need to add some water. Place the pot on the stove over high heat. Cover and bring to a boil again. Once it begins to boil, reduce the heat to medium-low. Give it a good stir, partially cover it, and ignore for at least 6 to 8 hours, preferably overnight. If you decide to go to bed, reduce the heat to low.

If you are awake, check on the stock occasionally. Keep a ladle and a small pot at arm's reach. Since the pot is simmering at medium-low, the liquid may begin to boil and rise to the upper edge of the pot. Should you find it is getting close to boiling over, you may want to remove some of the stock with a ladle. Be sure to put the excess stock in your storage container. Don't throw it away!

If you decide to go to bed and leave the stock going overnight on low heat (and I emphasize the lowest setting without the stove actually being turned off), you will not need to worry about any overflow or spillage from the stockpot.

8. Good morning! Turn the heat off and remove the pot from the stove. Place the colander over the storage container. Using the ladle, slowly remove the meat and herbs from the stock. Place these carefully into the colander. Once most of the meat is in the colander, slowly and carefully drain all the broth through the colander. Throw away all items in the colander (or give the meat, but not the bones, to your pets). Place the pot containing the stock in the refrigerator. Do not cover. Let cool all day or at least until a thick layer of fat solidifies on the top of the stock.

9. While still quite cold, remove this solidified layer of fat from the stock. Either throw it away or save it for something else down the road—soup, fried chicken livers, dumplings. It can be used! Your stock should have a consistency akin to Jell-O. If it doesn't, don't stress out. There was probably not enough marrow in the bones to do the trick. And now the stock is finished.

STOCKS AND THE RAFT

So you have stock. What do you do now?

You can use the stock now or cool it in an ice bath, whisking until the stock cools sufficiently for storage in the refrigerator. Alternatively, you could jar it following the instructions of your canning manual or freeze the stock in smaller portions; most of the recipes in this book call for 2 to 4 cups of stock.

If you find yourself with leftover stock and the opportunity to make more stock, add all of the old stock to the pot while making the new stock. This will enhance the flavor of the new batch.

Should you decide the stock isn't alluring enough and you want it to be clear and golden, just keep reading and you will be introduced to a wonderful, old, and quite amazing technique called the Raft! Then you will have clarified stock.

A raft is simply a mass of minced vegetables, egg whites, and eggshells, which floats on the surface of the soup. As it sits and the egg whites congeal, a small circular current forms in the stock below. This brings up all the impurities and minuscule solids from the stock. They adhere to the minced vegetables and eggshells and leave the stock clarified to a beautiful, golden-brown color. I learned this technique from the head chef of Cassis, a friend of mine, who told me some great secrets in food preparation. The next day I tried it and was so pleased with my results that now I must share the raft with you.

> 6 quarts stock, defatted but cloudy
> 12 egg whites, whisked
> 12 eggshells, cleaned and crushed
> 1 yellow onion, minced
> 2 carrots, shredded or chopped up very tiny
> 4 ribs celery, washed and minced

1. You will need a stockpot, a slotted spoon, some cheesecloth, a strainer, and a storage container that will fit in your refrigerator.

2. Put the defatted stock in the stockpot. There should be a considerable amount of space between the top of the pot and the top of the stock itself since no chicken or vegetables are floating in the mix. Place it on the stove, cover, and let it reach a boil. Be careful it doesn't overflow. The stock should remain at least 4 inches away from the top rim of the pot.

3. Place all the remaining ingredients in a large bowl, mix well, and set aside. Once the stock reaches a rolling boil, slide the contents out of the bowl onto the top of the stock. Do not stir.

4. Cover the stockpot again. Once it reaches a boil again, turn the heat down to medium-low. Let simmer for about 1 hour.

5. Remove the lid and carefully remove the raft—egg whites, shells, and vegetables—from the top of the stock. Place two layers of cheesecloth in the strainer and place the strainer over the storage container. Slowly pour the stock through the strainer. Discard any particles left in the cheesecloth.

6. If you want more intense flavor, place the clarified stock back on the stove and let it reduce by half.

You now have clarified stock. You can do a million and one things with this but for right now we are simply dealing with soup. Taste and adjust with salt or water. Do not add pepper! Ground pepper will ruin the effect. You will end up with floaters in your stock, which goes against the concept of a stock being clarified.

SPRING

FRENCH ONION SOUP

1 HOUR PREP TIME • YIELDS EIGHT 1-CUP SERVINGS

This is a light yet rich soup. I find using soy sauce and dark red wine (burgundy works best) hides the vegetarian nature of the soup. It shouldn't need salt, but if you or your guests feel it isn't salty enough, feel free to offer salt at the table.

> ¼ cup unsalted butter
> 2 pounds yellow onions, finely sliced
> ¼ cup soy sauce
> ¼ cup balsamic vinegar
> 1½ cups dry red wine or burgundy
> 2 bay leaves
> 4 cups Basic Vegetable Stock (page 31)
> Croutons
> Swiss or Gruyère cheese, grated

1. Melt the butter in a pot over high heat. Add the onions and mix well to coat them completely with the melted butter. Cover and let cook for 15 to 30 minutes.

2. Combine the soy sauce, balsamic vinegar, and red wine and set aside.

3. When the onions begin to stick to the bottom of the pot, have turned a dark golden brown, and begin to smell sweeter (almost like burnt sugar), add the bay leaves and the soy mixture.

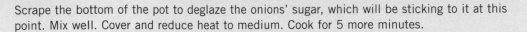

Scrape the bottom of the pot to deglaze the onions' sugar, which will be sticking to it at this point. Mix well. Cover and reduce heat to medium. Cook for 5 more minutes.

4. Add the stock to the onion mixture, mix well, cover, and let cook until the soup begins to simmer.

5. To serve, ladle the soup into soup crocks and cover them with the croutons and a nice layer of cheese. Place the crocks under the broiler and broil until the cheese forms a nice golden-brown crust on top of the soup. Make sure to tell your guests the bowls are quite hot and make sure you use oven mitts when handling the soup crocks once they are out of the oven.

SPRING

CREAM of ARTICHOKE SOUP with ROASTED GARLIC and NUTMEG

1 HOUR PREP TIME • YIELDS EIGHT 1-CUP SERVINGS

Nutmeg gives this soup a nice earthy feel to it. As you will notice, no other spices are used in this soup, so if you want to omit the nutmeg I suggest you add instead 2 bay leaves and 1 tea-spoon whole black peppercorns right after the onions and celery.

¼ cup unsalted butter

1 yellow onion, sliced

3 ribs celery, sliced, leaves included

Kosher salt

4 tablespoons flour

4 cups Basic Vegetable Stock (page 31) or Basic Chicken Stock (page 33)

Three 15-ounce cans artichoke hearts (not marinated), coarsely chopped, in two equal piles

1 head garlic, roasted (page 19)

White peppercorns, ground

2 cups cream

¼ cup cream sherry

¼ nutmeg seed, ground, plus more for garnish

Parmesan cheese, grated, for garnish

1. Melt the butter in a stockpot over medium-high heat. Add the onion, celery, and 1 teaspoon salt. Sauté until translucent.

2. Add the flour, stir well to coat onions and celery, then add the stock in 1-cup portions. Stir well after each addition to keep the flour from lumping up.

3. Add 1 pile of artichoke hearts, the roasted garlic, 1 teaspoon salt, and 1 teaspoon peppercorns. Stir well, cover, and allow the soup to come to a boil. Lower the heat to medium and simmer for 15 to 25 minutes.

4. Purée this in batches and strain into a storage container. Discard anything remaining in the strainer.

5. Wash out the stockpot. Pour the puréed soup back into it. Add the cream, sherry, nutmeg, and the second batch of chopped artichokes. Stir well. Cover and let simmer over medium-low heat until heated completely through.

6. Serve immediately with freshly grated parmesan and a little freshly grated nutmeg if you desire.

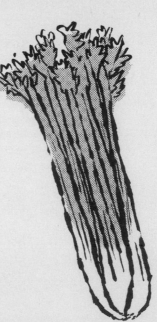

CREAM OF ASPARAGUS SOUP
1½ HOURS PREP TIME • YIELDS EIGHT 1-CUP SERVINGS

The time to make this soup is early spring when asparagus is in season and thus relatively inexpensive. If you want to omit the orange and nutmeg, go ahead.

1 large potato
2 tablespoons unsalted butter
1 yellow onion, finely sliced
Kosher salt
2 bay leaves, crumbled
2 pounds asparagus, 2-inch tips set aside and stems chopped
¼ bunch parsley, coarsely chopped
1 teaspoon black peppercorns, whole
½ cup dry white wine
4 cups Basic Vegetable Stock (page 31)
¼ teaspoon freshly grated nutmeg, plus more for garnish
Grated zest of 1 orange, plus more for garnish
White pepper, ground

1. Preheat the oven to 550°F.

2. Bake the potato until it is easily pierced with a fork, 45 minutes to 1 hour. Remove it from the oven and set aside to cool.

3. Melt the butter in a stockpot. Add the onion and 1 teaspoon salt and stir well. Cover and let simmer until golden. Add the bay leaves, the asparagus stems, and another teaspoon of salt.

4. Add the parsley and peppercorns, mix well, and add the wine and half of the stock. Cover and allow the stock to reach a boil. Lower the heat and let simmer for about 30 minutes, or until the asparagus begins to fall apart.

5. The baked potato should have cooled sufficiently to handle. Scrape the potato from the skin and place in a food processor. Purée the potato, adding a little vegetable stock, until it is creamy and thin. Remove from the food processor and set aside.

6. When the asparagus is ready, purée it in batches. Press it through a strainer. Discard any stringy fibers that may remain.

7. Pour the asparagus purée, the potato purée, the remaining vegetable stock, the grated nutmeg, and the orange zest into the stockpot. Whisk until everything is well incorporated. Set this aside while you steam the asparagus tips.

8. Fill a saucepan with 4 cups water and 1 tablespoon salt. Cover and let it reach a boil. When boiling, add the asparagus tips. Stir, cover, and blanch for about 2 minutes. Strain the asparagus tips using a colander.

9. Add the drained asparagus tips to the soup. Stir well, cover, and let it reach a simmer.

10. Remove from the heat and adjust the seasoning with salt and white pepper to taste.

11. To serve, garnish with freshly grated nutmeg and grated orange zest.

SAAG PANIR [CURRIED SPINACH SOUP WITH CHEESE AND BELL PEPPER]

3 HOURS [OVERNIGHT] PREP TIME • YIELDS TEN 1-CUP SERVINGS

This dense, rich soup is an adaptation of one of my favorite Indian dishes, *saag panir* (curried spinach with fresh cheese), and is perfect for chilly spring months when spinach is fresh. If you want to go all out, serve it with the Indian bread *naan* or *chapati*. To save time, you may substitute tofu for the fresh cheese—just fry half a pound of it as you would the cheese.

CHEESE

6 cups whole milk
¼ cup lemon juice
½ cup oil (peanut, coconut, or
   vegetable, not olive oil) or ghee
Flour, for dredging

SOUP

2 tablespoons oil (peanut, vegetable, or coconut) or ghee
2 tablespoons minced garlic
1 yellow onion, diced
Kosher salt
1-inch piece ginger, peeled and
   finely chopped

1 to 3 jalapeño, serrano, or Thai peppers, seeded and minced (optional)
2 tablespoons garam masala, purchased or homemade (recipe follows)
½ cup rice, toasted and ground
4 cups whey, saved from cheese-making process, or, if using tofu, water
2½ pounds fresh spinach
14-ounce can coconut milk
2 red bell peppers, stemmed, seeded, veins removed, and chopped
Fried cheese cubes (page 48) or fried tofu cubes
2 tablespoons lemon juice

GARAM MASALA
2 cinnamon sticks, broken
1 tablespoon cumin seeds
1 tablespoon coriander seeds
2 tablespoons black peppercorns
2 teaspoons cloves
2 tablespoon cardamom pods

1. To make the cheese, pour the milk into a stockpot. Turn the heat to high and leave uncovered. While waiting for the milk to reach a boil (about 30 minutes), place three layers of cheesecloth in a wire-mesh strainer and tape the cheesecloth around the edges so the hot cheese cannot pull it away from the mesh. Place the strainer over a storage container in order to save the liquid (whey) for the stock of the soup.

2. When the milk begins to boil, add the lemon juice and stir. In a few seconds the milk should begin to separate. The color will change from opaque white to a cloudy greenish-yellowish color. You should begin to find clumps of thick white stuff floating around in the pot. This is good! Take the pot off the burner and slowly pour the liquid through the cheesecloth-lined strainer. Once the soup pot is drained of liquid, wash it. Allow the whey to drip through the mesh until most of it has dripped. Pull the cheesecloth up around the cheese. Keep the strainer over the storage container. Carefully squeeze the cheesecloth-wrapped curds to get the rest of the water out. This will be very hot! Keep a bowl of ice water nearby. When you feel your fingers getting burned, cool them for a few minutes. Continue squeezing the curds until you have removed most of the excess water.

3. Place a large heavy, flat object on top of the cheesecloth-wrapped cheese and let it sit for at least 6 hours, overnight if possible. If you have room in your refrigerator, place the cheese with its weight there to cool down. (I like to turn a pie tin upside down, place the cheesecloth-wrapped cheese on top of it, place another pie tin right-side-up on top of it, and then place the weight in the top pie tin.)

4. When the cheese is very firm remove it from the pie tins. Pull off the cheesecloth and discard.

5. Heat the oil in a small pot until hot enough for frying. Cut the cheese into ½-inch cubes. Dredge the cubes in flour so they will not stick together. In batches, carefully place the cubes in the oil and fry until golden brown. Remove from the oil and place on a paper towel to soak up any excess grease. Set aside.

6. To make the garam masala, place a heavy-bottomed skillet over high heat. Once hot, add cinnamon sticks. Toast and remove. Repeat with cumin, coriander, black peppercorns, cloves, and cardamom pods, toasting each spice individually. Once all the spices are toasted, grind them together in a coffee mill or spice mill to a fine powder. Keep sealed in a dark, cool area until ready to use.

7. To make the soup, heat the oil in a soup pot. Add the garlic and sauté until golden. Add the onion and stir well. Add 1 tablespoon salt and stir again. Cover and let simmer for 5 minutes, or until the onion is translucent. Add the ginger and the peppers and mix well. Cover and let simmer for 5 minutes.

8. Add the garam masala and ground rice and mix well. Add 1 cup of the reserved whey or water. Mix well, cover, and let cook for 10 minutes.

9. Add the spinach in four batches. After each batch stir to mix well, cover, and let the spinach reduce.

10. Once all of the spinach has decreased in size, add 3 more cups of whey and stir well. Cover and let reach a boil. Reduce the heat to medium and let simmer for 20 minutes.

11. Purée the soup in batches. Press through a strainer into a storage container. Discard any lumps left in the strainer.

12. Wash out the soup pot. Place the soup back in the pot. Add the coconut milk, red bell peppers, and fried cheese. Place back on the stove, cover, and let simmer over medium heat for about 15 minutes.

13. Remove from the heat and add the lemon juice. Serve immediately.

ROASTED GARLIC SOUP WITH CROUTONS AND GRUYÈRE

2 HOURS PREP TIME • YIELDS EIGHT 1-CUP SERVINGS

Because garlic is always available, you can make this soup year round. I suggest making it in the spring when the weather is beginning to change, since garlic is good for both the blood and for fighting off colds and the flu.

3 slices stale bread, cut into approximately ½-inch cubes
2 tablespoons olive oil
1 tablespoon fresh marjoram leaves and stems, chopped
1 tablespoon fresh rosemary leaves, chopped
1 tablespoon fresh savory leaves and stems, chopped
1 tablespoon fresh tarragon leaves and stems, chopped
1 tablespoon fresh thyme leaves and stems, chopped
1 tablespoon fresh oregano leaves and stems, chopped
3 to 5 heads garlic, roasted and puréed (page 19)
2 bay leaves
1 teaspoon black peppercorns
Kosher salt
1 cup dry white wine
8 cups Basic Vegetable Stock (page 31)
4 cups cream
8 ounces Gruyère cheese, grated, for garnish

1. Preheat the oven to 550°F.

2. Toss the bread cubes with 2 tablespoons of the olive oil. Spread them out on a baking sheet and toast until golden and crispy, 5 to 10 minutes.

3. Add the herbs, the puréed garlic, bay leaves, peppercorns, a pinch of salt, the wine, and the stock to the soup pot. Mix well and let it reach a boil over medium-high heat. Once boiling, lower the heat to medium-low and let simmer for about 30 minutes.

4. Pour the soup slowly through a strainer and into a storage container. Discard the herbs from the strainer. Clean out the soup pot. Refill with the strained soup. Add the cream, stir well, and let the soup reach a simmer.

5. Serve topped with a few croutons and a nice portion of grated Gruyère cheese.

CURRIED AVOCADO SOUP
1½ HOURS PREP TIME • YIELDS EIGHT 1-CUP SERVINGS

This sweet and spicy soup is best served in spring when avocados are abundant, ripe, and, best of all, inexpensive. You may omit or cut down the number of the peppers if you want to make the soup milder.

3 ripe avocados
14-ounce can coconut milk
2 tablespoons oil (coconut, peanut, or avocado) or ghee
1 tablespoon minced garlic
1 yellow onion, diced
2 teaspoons kosher salt
1 teaspoon coriander seeds, toasted and coarsely ground
3 to 5 jalapeño, serrano, or Thai peppers
1-inch piece ginger, peeled and minced
1 cup shredded unsweetened coconut, lightly toasted, plus extra for garnish
1 ripe mango, peeled and chopped
¼ pineapple, peeled, cored, and finely chopped
½ teaspoon turmeric
2 tablespoons lemon juice
Cilantro, washed and chopped, for garnish

1. Peel, pit, and purée the avocados in a food processor until smooth. (If necessary, add a little coconut milk to thin.) Scrape down the sides occasionally to get the lumps of avocado incorporated into the rest of the purée. Push this through a strainer to make sure the texture is smooth. Add the coconut milk and enough water to thin the puréed avocados to the consistency of pancake batter. Set aside.

2. Place the oil in a soup pot and set it on the stove over high heat. Add the garlic and stir well. Once the garlic starts to turn golden brown, add the onion and 1 teaspoon salt and stir well. Cover and lower heat to medium-high. Let cook for 5 minutes, or until the onion becomes translucent.

3. Add the coriander, peppers, and ginger. Mix well, cover, and let simmer for another 10 minutes.

4. Add the coconut, mango, pineapple, turmeric, and 1 teaspoon salt. Stir well, cover, and let simmer for 15 more minutes.

5. Once this mixture is steaming and bubbling, add the avocado purée. Stir to incorporate and turn the heat down to medium-low. Cover and let cook until heated through. Remove from heat and add the lemon juice. Stir well.

6. Serve topped with cilantro and/or toasted shredded coconut.

A very light and velvety soup with a fresh and zesty flavor, this soup is perfect for a chilly spring afternoon. If you want to make it vegan you can use canola or vegetable oil instead of butter.

2 tablespoons unsalted butter
1 yellow onion, thinly sliced
2-inch piece ginger, peeled and minced
Pinch cayenne pepper
Kosher salt
1½ pounds carrots, grated
6 cups Basic Vegetable Stock (page 31)
8-ounce can orange juice concentrate
White peppercorns, ground
Sesame oil and/or sliced green onions, for garnish

1. Melt the butter in a stockpot over high heat. Add the onion and sauté until translucent and tender. Add the ginger, cayenne, and 1 teaspoon salt and stir well. Cover and let cook for about 5 minutes, or until the onion begins to release its juice.

2. Add the shredded carrots, in batches. Add another teaspoon of salt and mix well. Add enough stock to reach the top of the carrots. Cover and let simmer on medium-high heat for 15 to 20 minutes.

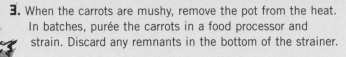

3. When the carrots are mushy, remove the pot from the heat. In batches, purée the carrots in a food processor and strain. Discard any remnants in the bottom of the strainer.

4. Rinse the stockpot thoroughly and return the puréed carrots to it. Add the orange juice concentrate. If the soup is thick, add some water. Adjust to taste with salt and white pepper. The soup should be slightly sweet and tangy.

5. When serving this soup I like to add a splash of sesame oil and/or freshly sliced green onions to the top.

CHICKEN and LEMON SOUP with RICE
1 HOUR PREP TIME • YIELDS TWELVE 1-CUP SERVINGS

This is a spring soup because dill is a very prevalent herb this time of year. It is a light and refreshing soup with a Grecian ancestry.

8 cups Basic Chicken Stock, clarified (page 33)
3 egg yolks
¼ cup lemon juice
1 teaspoon kosher salt
1 teaspoon white peppercorns, ground
¼ cup dry white wine
½ cup basmati rice, washed and soaked for about 15 minutes
Fresh dill, chopped, for garnish

1. Take 1 cup of the chicken stock and set it aside. Place the rest of the chicken stock in a stockpot and set it over medium-high heat. Let it reach a boil. Lower the heat to medium-low and cover.

2. Whisk the egg yolks, lemon juice, salt, peppercorns, and wine together. While whisking, slowly add ½ cup of the simmering broth to the egg mixture. (You do not want the eggs to scramble and become solid lumps.) Then, whisking the stock all the while, pour the egg mixture into the pot. Turn off the heat and set the stockpot aside.

3. Take the reserved cup of stock and pour it into a 1-quart saucepan. Place over high heat, cover, and let it reach a boil. Add the rice to the boiling stock. Turn the heat down to low, cover, and let cook for 18 to 20 minutes. Don't lift the lid—just leave the rice to do its thing. Remove the pot from the heat and let it cool down.

4. To serve, place a scoop of rice in the bottom of each bowl. Cover it with hot soup and top with chopped dill.

This lovely pale green French soup is a perfect choice for chilly spring afternoons. Fresh spring peas and the earthy tartness of arugula really make this soup taste hearty while it remains relatively light and fresh.

2 tablespoons unsalted butter	6 cups boiling water
½ head garlic, minced	1 teaspoon kosher salt
½ cup arugula	2 cups lima beans, frozen and thawed
¼ cup basil	or fresh
¼ cup curly parsley	1 cup spring peas, fresh or frozen
1 egg yolk	2 yellow onions, finely chopped
½ cup grated parmesan cheese	6 small zucchini, grated
¼ cup pine nuts, toasted	1 cup dry white wine
½ cup olive oil	

1. Place the butter, garlic, arugula, basil, parsley, egg yolk, parmesan, and pine nuts in a food processor. Purée until they form a thick paste. With the food processor still running, slowly pour in ¼ cup of the olive oil until the mixture has a thick mayonnaise-like consistency. Set aside.

2. Pour the water and salt into a soup pot and place over high heat. When the water begins to boil, add the lima beans and stir a couple of times. Cover and allow the beans to soften, about 20 minutes. Add the peas and cook, uncovered, for 10 minutes. Don't cook any longer, otherwise you will lose the vibrant green color of the peas. Purée the contents of the pot and press through a strainer. Discard what remains in the strainer. Set aside.

3. Rinse the soup pot thoroughly. Heat the remaining oil in the soup pot over high heat. Add the onions. Stir, cover, and sauté until the onions are tender and translucent. Add the zucchini, stir well, and sauté for about 5 minutes, or until it is soft, but still has texture. Add the wine, stir, reduce the heat to medium, cover, and simmer for a few minutes.

4. Add the puréed vegetables to the pot. Stir, lower the heat to low, cover, and allow to come to a simmer.

5. Ladle the simmering soup into soup bowls. Add a good dollop of the arugula-basil pesto to the top of the soup and serve immediately.

TAFFY'S PEPPER POT
45 MINUTES TO 1 HOUR PREP TIME • YIELDS SIX 1-CUP SERVINGS

Taffy is an old and hopefully outdated nickname of mine. The main ingredients of this soup are peppers—lots of them: Anaheims, jalapeños, poblanos, Thai, habañeros, Chinese long, and bells. Needless to say, this soup can be extremely spicy hot—so warn your guests and rate the soup as five stars on the heat scale. This soup is pretty hot on the first day you make it but it might be akin to magma after sitting in your fridge for 3 days. If you have a cold, eat this soup, and the cold, along with anything else in your sinuses, will swiftly go away!

¼ cup sesame oil
8 cloves garlic, thinly sliced
1 yellow onion, sliced
½ red bell pepper, stemmed, seeded, and sliced
½ yellow bell pepper, stemmed, seeded, and sliced
½ orange bell pepper, stemmed, seeded, and sliced
1 Anaheim pepper, stemmed, seeded, and sliced
1 jalapeño pepper, stemmed, seeded, and sliced
2 to 4 Thai peppers, sliced into ¼-inch rings
1 habañero or Scotch bonnet pepper, sliced into ¼-inch rings (optional)
2 to 4 Chinese long peppers, sliced into ¼-inch rings
1 poblano pepper, stemmed, seeded, and sliced
8 cups clarified chicken or vegetable stock (page 37)
Rice or bread, for serving

1. Pour the oil into a soup pot. Set the pot over high heat. When you see the first signs of smoke rising, add the garlic and stir it quickly to coat with oil. When the garlic begins to change from white to gold in color, add the onion. Stir again to coat with oil. Reduce the temperature to medium-high, cover the pot, and allow the onions to sauté until they grow tender. Add all the peppers. Stir well to coat with oil, cover, and allow the peppers to soften.

2. Once the peppers have grown slightly soft, pour the stock into the pot. Stir well, cover, and reduce the heat to medium-low. Allow the soup to come to a simmer. Remove from the heat and serve with rice or bread. (If you plan on making this soup in large batches, remember that peppers grow hotter the longer they sit.)

MOLE VERDE CON POLLO
1 TO 1½ HOURS PREP TIME • YIELDS FOUR TO EIGHT 1-CUP SERVINGS

This mole has a delightful zesty kick and bites back. It uses tomatillos instead of regular red tomatoes. They have a lovely acidic flavor that blends really well with the tequila, peppers, cilantro, and lime. Just remember to warn your guests beforehand that it is very spicy. I highly recommend taking a few minutes and making a red pepper coulis (page 64) to swirl on the top of this pale green soup. The contrast in colors is quite amazing!

2 pounds tomatillos, washed well and papery skins removed

4 jalapeño peppers, stems removed

1 to 2 pounds skinless and boneless chicken breast

4 cups Basic Chicken Stock (page 33)

¼ cup tequila (the cheaper the better)

¼ cup olive oil or corn oil

2 tablespoons minced garlic

1 yellow onion, thinly sliced

2 zucchini, cut lengthwise and very thinly sliced

1 tablespoon kosher salt

1 tablespoon cumin seeds, roasted and ground

1 tablespoon minced fresh sage

1 tablespoon minced fresh oregano

1 tablespoon cracked black peppercorns

1 cup heavy cream

¼ cup lime juice

1 cup roasted, peeled, destemmed, deveined, and chopped fresh Hatch green chilies

2 tablespoons coarsely chopped fresh cilantro

Red Bell Pepper Coulis (recipe follows)

1. Preheat the oven to 550°F.

2. Place the tomatillos and the jalapeños in an ovenproof roasting pan and roast for about 30 minutes, or until the skin of the tomatillos is brown, juice is exuding from them, and they are extremely tender, and the skin of the jalapeños is shriveled and turning brown. Remove the roasting pan from the oven and set it aside until the tomatillos and jalapeños are cool enough to handle.

3. Place the chicken breasts, stock, and tequila in another roasting pan or baking dish. Make sure that the chicken is completely covered. If you need more stock or tequila, use it! You will just have more soup afterwards. Cover the dish with a lid or aluminum foil and place in the oven. Cook for 40 minutes, or until the chicken is white throughout. You may cook the chicken at the same time you roast the tomatillos, just not in the same container. Once cooked through, turn off the oven, remove the chicken from the broth, and set the broth aside. There should be a heady and slightly sweet odor emanating from the broth. That is the tequila. The alcohol has cooked off but the flavor has remained. Once the chicken is cool enough to handle, take it between your hands and shred it by rubbing your hands back and forth. Place the shredded chicken on a plate and set aside.

4. Place a soup pot over medium-high heat and add the oil. Add the garlic and sauté until garlic begins to turn golden. Add the onion, stir well to coat with the oil and garlic, cover, and sauté until the onion begins to turn translucent. Add the zucchini, salt, cumin, sage, oregano, and peppercorns. Stir well again and cover. Lower the heat to medium. Check and stir occasionally to make sure nothing is burning at the bottom of the pot.

5. In batches if necessary, place the tomatillos and jalapeños in a food processor and purée until smooth. Pour through a strainer and discard any skins and seeds. When finished, add the cream, chicken broth, lime juice, and diced green chilies, and whisk well. Set aside.

6. The zucchini should be tender and there should be a nice liquid forming in the soup pot. At this point, add the shredded chicken. Stir well and then add the puréed tomatillos. Stir again, cover, and let the soup simmer over low heat for 5 minutes.

7. Remove the soup from the heat, add the chopped cilantro, stir well, and serve.

RED BELL PEPPER COULIS
MAKES ABOUT 2 CUPS

Roast 1 head of garlic (page 19), squeeze out the garlic cloves, and place in a food processor. Add a 1-pound jar of drained roasted red peppers and ½ teaspoon salt. Purée until completely smooth. Pour the purée through a fine mesh strainer. Adjust the flavor with salt if needed. Pour the coulis into a squeeze bottle and make a spiral of vibrant red on top of the pale green soup. Or, if you don't have a squeeze bottle, a spoonful will do just fine.

I read a while back that chanterelles and grapes worked well together so I decided to try to experiment with a small batch of soup. Of course, I was kind of worried that people might raise an eyebrow at the idea of eating a hot grape submerged in a soup, but when I tasted the soup for the first time, I was impressed. Only after my first taste did I realize that the soup needed something to balance out the sweetness of the grapes, balsamic vinegar, and the caramelized onions—goat cheese was the only thing I could see working. Suffice it to say, a few customers did raise an eyebrow, but they were more than pleasantly surprised at the unusual combination of flavors laid out before them.

4 tablespoons unsalted butter
1 yellow onion, thinly sliced
4 medium shallots, peeled and quartered
4 tablespoons balsamic vinegar
1 cup red seedless grapes, washed and halved
2 tablespoons minced fresh rosemary
½ cup tawny port
8 ounces chanterelle mushrooms, thinly sliced
1 tablespoon kosher salt
1 tablespoon cracked black peppercorns
1 pound red new potatoes thinly sliced
8 cups Basic Vegetable Stock (page 31)
Chèvre (goat cheese)

SPRING

1. Melt 2 tablespoons of the butter in a soup pot over high heat. Add the onion and shallots, stir well to glaze with butter, cover, and allow to caramelize. Stir occasionally to keep them from sticking to the bottom of the pot. When they begin to caramelize, add 2 tablespoons of the balsamic vinegar to the pot and stir well. Cover and allow the onion and shallots to cook for a few more minutes.

2. Add the grapes, rosemary, and wine. Stir again, cover, and lower the heat. Simmer for a few minutes, or until the grapes are heated all the way through. Do not let the grapes break down or turn to mush. Remove the mixture from the pot and set aside.

3. Return the heat to high and add the remaining 2 tablespoons of butter to the pot. When it has melted, add the mushrooms. Stir well, cover, and allow the mushrooms to sauté until they begin to release their juices. Add the remaining balsamic vinegar, salt, and peppercorns. Cover and allow to sauté for 2 to 3 more minutes.

4. Add the potatoes and stock. Stir well to evenly blend the ingredients. Cover and allow the soup to reach a boil. Reduce the heat to medium and simmer until the potatoes are al dente to tender, about 15 minutes.

5. Remove the soup pot from the heat. Add the caramelized onion mixture and stir well. Adjust to taste with salt and pepper. Garnish each serving with a small dollop of chèvre.

This soup is similar to Tomato Rasam (page 97), yet different enough that I had to include it. The one thing I love about this soup is that it contains the surprise of cucumber. I had never served cooked cucumbers before this soup and I never expected that I would; however, this soup proved me happily wrong. Strange, but simple and delicate.

Water
1½ cups yellow lentils
¼ teaspoon turmeric
1 teaspoon cumin seeds, toasted and ground
2 teaspoons black peppercorns, toasted and ground
2 tablespoons tamarind paste or lemon juice
2 cucumbers, peeled, seeded, and thinly sliced
2 teaspoons kosher salt
2 tablespoons ghee, canola, or peanut oil
1 teaspoon black mustard seeds
½ teaspoon asafetida
4 jalapeño, serrano, or Thai peppers, chopped
24 curry leaves, dried or fresh (optional)
¼ cup chopped cilantro

1. Heat 8 cups of water in a soup pot. When it reaches a boil, add the lentils and the turmeric. Stir well to keep the lentils from clumping. Cover, leaving the lid ajar. Cook the lentils for

20 to 45 minutes, or until done. Remove from heat and pour through a strainer. Discard the water and set the lentils aside.

2. Clean out the soup pot. Pour the lentils back into the pot and add the cumin, pepper, and 5 cups of water. If you are using tamarind paste, add it now. Stir well to make sure any lumps in the paste are broken up. Bring to a boil, cover, reduce the heat to medium-low, and allow to simmer for 5 minutes. Add the sliced cucumbers and stir well. Cover and allow to simmer for another 5 minutes.

3. Remove from the heat and add the lemon juice, if using, and salt. Stir well, cover, and set aside.

4. Heat the ghee in a saucepan. Once it is very hot, add the mustard seeds. Cover the pan quickly to keep the seeds from spattering all over your kitchen. Add the asafetida and give the pan a quick shake. Add the peppers to the pan and sauté until the skins begin to blister and crack. Carefully add the curry leaves, if using. Be forewarned: They make a lot of noise and you may be startled when placing them in the hot oil. Quickly fry them, then remove the saucepan from the heat.

5. With one hand holding the saucepan, add its contents to the soup while with the other hand you hold the lid over the soup pot—just in case the oil spits and spatters when hitting the water in the soup. Stir well to incorporate the spices and top with cilantro. Serve immediately.

Here is a nice little soup you can make if you find yourself with leftover crab. Yeah right, like there would ever be leftover crab! Seriously, I do like the gentle hint of citrus, which infuses the entire soup with a refreshing taste. The Tabasco is a nice Southern touch—its vinegary zest and bite works perfectly with the soup's overall light flavor. The best part is that this soup is very easy to make!

1 large baking potato
¼ cup unsalted butter
1 yellow onion, finely sliced
1 rib celery, minced
1 tablespoon kosher salt
1 teaspoon black peppercorns, toasted and coarsely ground
¼ cup dry white wine
1 bay leaf, crumbled
2 pounds flaked crab, or 1 pound crab and 1 pound imitation crab
4 cups Basic Vegetable Stock (page 31) or Basic Fish Stock (page 29) or crab stock
1 cup heavy cream
2 teaspoons coriander seeds, toasted and ground
Grated zest of 1 orange and 1 lemon
Chives or green onions
Tabasco

SPRING

1. Preheat the oven to 550°F.

2. Place the potato in the oven and bake until it is easily pierced with a fork, 45 minutes to 1 hour. Remove it from the oven and set aside to cool.

3. Once cool enough to handle, slice the potato in half, scoop the meat out, and discard the skin. Purée in a food processor until there are no lumps. Remove the puréed potato from the food processor and set aside.

4. Melt the butter in a soup pot over medium-high heat. Add the onion and celery and stir well. Cover, and allow to sauté until the onion is translucent and the celery is tender.

5. Add the salt, peppercorns, wine, bay leaf, and 1 pound of the crab. If you are using half real and half fake crab, use the fake crab now. Stir well, cover, and allow to simmer over medium heat for a few minutes. Add the stock, cover, and cook for about 30 minutes, or until the celery becomes mushy and the crab is very tender.

6. Remove the pot from the heat and, in batches, purée in the food processor and place in a bowl until all of the soup is puréed. Do not press the soup through a sieve or pour through a strainer. Clean out the pot and then pour the purée back into it. Add the rest of the crab, potato purée, cream, coriander, and orange and lemon zest. Allow the bisque to simmer over medium-low heat until it is heated throughout. Stir occasionally to make sure the flavors are blended. Adjust flavor with salt and pepper if necessary. Serve immediately with fresh chopped chives or green onions, and/or Tabasco.

This soup is a variation of the Corn and Green Chile Chowder (page 150). Although similar, the different choice of chilies completely changes the flavor, color, and heat of the soup. You can use a variety of different dried chilies in combination or by themselves. When I first started making this soup, I only used chipotles. Now I use a blend of ancho chilies and chipotles for a smoky, sweet, and hot flavor combination. If you decide to try other chilies, go right ahead and experiment. Just keep the proportions the same.

2 pounds new red potatoes, washed and diced

Olive oil

4 dried chipotles chilies

4 dried ancho chilies

4 cups boiling water

¼ cup unsalted butter

2 tablespoons minced garlic

1 yellow onion, diced small

1 rib celery, sliced lengthwise and diced

1 tablespoon minced fresh sage

1 tablespoon minced fresh thyme

1 tablespoon minced fresh oregano

1 tablespoon cumin seeds, roasted and minced

1 tablespoon kosher salt

¼ cup flour

2 cups Basic Vegetable Stock (page 31)

2 cups milk

2 ears of corn, washed and silk removed

1 cup heavy cream

1. Preheat the oven to 550°F.

2. Sprinkle the potatoes with a little olive oil and spread out on a tray. Bake for about 20 minutes, or until the potatoes are tender but not mushy. Remove from the oven and set aside.

3. Remove the stems and seeds of the chilies. Open the chilies so that they can get plenty of water on all sides of them. Place them in a stainless steel or glass bowl and pour the boiling water over them. Place a plate over the chilies to make sure that they remain submerged. Quickly cover the bowl with plastic wrap so that the heat remains inside the bowl and let stand for 30 minutes. Remove the plastic wrap and carefully place the hot chilies in a food processor. Purée the chilies to a smooth paste. Use some of the water if necessary. Pour the purée through a strainer into a bowl. Discard any remains. Set aside.

4. Heat the butter in a soup pot over medium-high heat until it has completely melted. Add the garlic, stir well, cover, and allow to sauté until the garlic turns golden. Add the onion and celery. Stir well, cover, and allow to sauté until the onion becomes translucent. Add all the spices, the chile paste, and the salt. Stir well again, cover, and simmer for a few minutes to help evenly distribute the flavor of the spices.

5. Add the flour and quickly stir into the liquid that has formed in the soup pot. Make sure that all lumps are broken up and there is no remaining dry flour on the sides of the pot. Add the stock. Stir this enough so that the flour and butter paste evenly thins throughout the soup pot. Make sure that you stir from the bottom of the pot so as not to burn or cause it to stick. Add the potatoes and milk. Stir well. Cover and allow the soup to simmer for a few minutes over medium-low heat.

6. Stand each ear of corn on its wider end. Carefully slice the kernels off the ears. Discard the cobs and add the corn to the pot. Add the cream. Stir well to incorporate, cover, and allow to simmer for a few more minutes until the corn is heated through. Remove from heat and serve immediately.

SUMMER

TOMATO and SALMON BISQUE
1 HOUR PREP TIME • YIELDS EIGHT 1-CUP SERVINGS

This is a light soup . . . really it is! Early summer through early fall would be the best time to prepare it—when the salmon is in season and therefore less expensive.

¼ cup unsalted butter
1 tablespoon minced garlic
1 yellow onion, thinly sliced
1 pound shallots, thinly sliced
1 teaspoon black peppercorns
½ cup dry white wine
2 bay leaves, crumbled
¼ bunch dill, coarsely chopped
¼ bunch tarragon, coarsely chopped
12 to 15 medium Roma tomatoes, peeled, seeded, and chopped (page 23), or
   32-ounce can diced tomatoes
Kosher salt
1½ pounds fresh salmon, cut into ½-inch cubes and divided in two piles—
   1 pound and ½ pound
4 cups Basic Vegetable Stock (page 31)
Zest of 1 orange
Fresh dill or curls of orange zest, for garnish

1. Melt the butter in a stockpot over medium-high heat. Add the garlic and sauté until golden. Add the onion and shallots and stir to coat with butter. Cover and let cook until translucent.

2. Add the peppercorns, wine, bay leaves, dill, tarragon, and half of the tomatoes. Stir well to incorporate ingredients. Cover and let simmer for 10 minutes, or until the mixture starts to boil.

3. Add 2 teaspoons salt, 1 pound of the salmon, and 2 cups of the stock. Stir well, cover, and let this simmer until the salmon completely flakes apart. Purée in batches. Do not strain.

4. Pour the soup back in the pot. Add the orange zest, the rest of the tomatoes, salmon, and stock. Stir well, cover, and let simmer over medium-low heat for 20 minutes, or until the salmon is cooked through. Stir occasionally to keep the bottom from burning.

5. Adjust to taste with salt, peppercorns, wine, or stock.

6. To serve, garnish with a sprig of dill or curls of orange zest.

CURRIED SUMMER SQUASH SOUP WITH TOMATO AND CILANTRO

2 HOURS PREP TIME • YIELDS EIGHT 1-CUP SERVINGS

This is a light and refreshing summer soup. I like to use the long, yellow, bottleneck variety of summer squash. However, the scalloped Sunburst variety also works quite nicely. If you want to omit the peppers, feel free.

¼ cup canola or coconut oil or ghee
1 tablespoon minced garlic
1 yellow onion, finely sliced
Kosher salt
1-inch piece of ginger, peeled and minced
1 tablespoon curry powder
4 cups Basic Vegetable Stock (page 31)
1½ to 2 pounds yellow summer squash, 1 to 1½ pounds shredded and ½ pound
   sliced ⅛ to ¼ inch thick
14-ounce can coconut milk
3 to 5 jalapeño, serrano, or Thai peppers, sliced
1 pound new red potatoes, washed and sliced ¼ inch thick
2 tablespoons lemon juice
Diced tomatoes and cilantro leaves, for garnish

1. Heat the oil or melt the ghee in a soup pot over medium-high heat. Add the garlic and sauté until golden. Add the onion and 1 teaspoon salt. Stir well, cover, and cook until the onion is between translucent and golden in color.

2. Add the ginger, stir well, and let cook for 5 minutes. Add the curry powder and 1 cup of the stock and stir again. Cover and cook for 10 minutes.

3. Add the shredded squash, the rest of the stock, and 1 teaspoon salt. Stir well, cover, and cook until the squash is very mushy, about 30 minutes.

4. Purée the soup in batches and strain into a storage container until all soup has been puréed. Discard anything that remains in the strainer.

5. Clean out the stockpot and place back on the stove. Return the puréed soup to the soup pot. Add the coconut milk, sliced squash, peppers, and potatoes to the soup. Stir well, cover, and let simmer over medium heat until the potatoes are tender and easily pierced with a fork Stir occasionally to keep the soup from scorching. Remove from the heat, add the lemon juice, and stir well.

6. Transfer to bowls and garnish with diced tomatoes and a few leaves of cilantro.

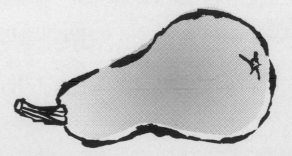

SUMMER

TOMATO BISQUE with ROASTED GARLIC, SAFFRON, and ORANGE

1½ HOURS PREP TIME • YIELDS TEN TO TWELVE 1-CUP SERVINGS

The perfect soup to make when tomatoes are in season—orange lifts the soup, saffron perfumes it, and cream cheese gives it a decadent velvety texture. If you don't want the soup to be too sweet, omit the wine or cut it back to ¼ cup at first, then adjust until you find the right sweetness.

¼ cup unsalted butter
2 shallots, peeled and sliced
1 red onion, sliced
½ cup sweet red wine (optional)
2 bay leaves, crumbled
1 teaspoon black peppercorns
Kosher salt
12 to 15 medium Roma tomatoes, peeled, seeded, and chopped (page 23), or 32-ounce can diced tomatoes
4 cups Basic Vegetable Stock (page 31) or Basic Chicken Stock (page 33)
1 head garlic, roasted and puréed (page 19)
8 to 10 threads saffron, in ¼ cup boiling water
8 ounces cream cheese
Grated zest and juice of 2 oranges

1. Melt the butter in a stockpot. Add the shallots and onion. Mix well, cover, and let cook for 15 minutes, or until the onion and shallots are just beginning to caramelize.

2. Add the wine, or water if you don't want to use wine. Mix well, cover, and simmer for 5 minutes.

3. Add the bay leaves, peppercorns, salt to taste, and half of the diced tomatoes. Mix well, cover, and simmer for 10 minutes. Add the stock. Cover and cook for 30 minutes.

4. Purée the soup in batches. Strain batches into the storage container until all the soup has been puréed. Discard anything that remains in the strainer and wash out the stockpot.

5. Place the puréed garlic, the saffron in water, and the cream cheese in the food processor. Purée to an even, smooth, and very yellow paste. Stir the paste into the soup.

6. Fill the stockpot with the garlic, cream cheese, and saffron soup, add the rest of the tomatoes and simmer over medium-low heat. If the soup is too thick, add another cup of stock. Stir occasionally to keep the soup from burning to the bottom of the pot. Cover and let cook until the tomatoes are heated through and you can see steam rising from the surface.

7. Remove from the heat, add both the zest and juice of the oranges, and serve immediately.

CHANTERELLE BISQUE WITH TOASTED PECANS

1½ HOURS PREP TIME • YIELDS EIGHT 1-CUP SERVINGS

I suggest making this soup when chanterelle mushrooms are at their best—late summer through early fall. The soup is lovely served with chopped and toasted pecans sprinkled on top of it.

4 tablespoons unsalted butter
1 yellow onion, chopped
2 ribs celery, chopped
Kosher salt
2 bay leaves, crumbled
1 tablespoon minced fresh rosemary
1 teaspoon black peppercorns
1 pound chanterelle mushrooms, wiped clean and sliced
2 cups Basic Vegetable Stock (page 31) or Basic Chicken Stock (page 33)
2 tablespoons roasted garlic purée (page 19)
2 cups milk
1 cup cream
2 large shallots, thinly sliced
¼ cups cream sherry
½ cup pecans, toasted and coarsely chopped

1. Melt 2 tablespoons of the butter in a stockpot over medium-high heat. Add the onion and sauté until golden. Add the celery and 1 teaspoon salt. Stir well, cover, and cook until the onion is translucent and the celery begins to release its juices. Add the bay leaves, rosemary, and peppercorns. Stir well, cover, and allow to simmer for 5 minutes, or until a nice amount of liquid has formed.

2. Add roughly ¾ pound of the mushrooms and 1 teaspoon salt. Mix well and cover. Let cook until the mushrooms are reduced by half.

3. Add the stock. Cover and let cook for 30 minutes on medium heat. Stir occasionally to keep the bottom from burning.

4. Remove the pot from the heat. In batches, purée and strain the contents of the soup pot into a storage container. Add the roasted garlic purée, milk, and cream, stir well, and set aside. Discard anything remaining in the strainer.

5. Clean the stockpot and place it back on the heat. Melt the rest of the butter over medium-high heat. Add the shallots and the rest of the mushrooms. Stir well and cover. Let simmer for 10 minutes, or until the mushrooms have reduced in size and the shallots have become tender.

6. Add the sherry and stir until evenly distributed. Add the reserved soup. Stir well and cover. Simmer over medium-low heat for 5 to 10 minutes.

7. Toast the pecans in an oven set at 550°F for 5 minutes, or until you can smell them. The instant you smell the pecans, remove them. Allow the nuts to cool, then coarsely chop them into smaller pieces.

8. Ladle the soup into bowls and serve immediately, topped with pecans.

ZUCCHINI with DILL SOUP

1 HOUR PREP TIME • YIELDS EIGHT 1-CUP SERVINGS

Though this rich soup has quite a bit of intense flavor, it doesn't seem all that heavy, even with potatoes in it. Dill lightens the flavor. This soup came to me when I found myself with a couple of dozen zucchini sitting around.

¼ cup unsalted butter
1 tablespoon minced garlic
1 yellow onion, thinly sliced
Kosher salt
1 teaspoon peppercorns, cracked
3 tablespoons coarsely chopped fresh dill
2 bay leaves, crumbled
½ cup white wine
3 zucchini, thinly sliced
4 cups Basic Vegetable Stock (page 31) or Basic Chicken Stock (page 33)
1 pound potatoes, red or Yukon gold, washed and thinly sliced
Sour cream and fresh dill, for garnish (optional)

1. Melt the butter in a stockpot over medium-high heat. Add the minced garlic and sauté until golden. Add the onion and 1 teaspoon salt. Mix well and cover. Let cook until the onion is soft and its liquid is released.

2. Add the peppercorns, dill, bay leaves, and white wine and stir well. At this point the mixture should resemble more of a rich wine sauce than a soup. Cover and let simmer for 10 minutes.

3. Add the zucchini and 1 teaspoon salt and mix well. Cover and allow to simmer for another 10 minutes.

4. Add the stock and the potatoes. Mix well, cover, and allow the soup to reach a boil. Once it boils, lower the heat to medium and cook until the potatoes can be pierced easily with a fork.

5. Remove from the heat and serve immediately. You may garnish this soup with a dollop of sour cream and a little more chopped fresh dill if you so desire.

SUMMER

CURRIED PEANUT SOUP WITH GREEN ONIONS

1½ HOURS PREP TIME • YIELDS EIGHT 1-CUP SERVINGS

This soup can be made anytime of the year, of course. But it seems to me summertime is the perfect time for this light and thin soup that has a minimal amount of stuff in it yet can make one sweat a bit. So get the perspiration going and chill your body for a little while!

    1 teaspoon turmeric
    ½ stick cinnamon
    10 cloves
    10 cardamom pods
    10 black peppercorns
    ¼ teaspoon cumin seeds
    ½ teaspoon coriander seeds
    2 tablespoons peanut oil
    1 teaspoon brown mustard seeds
    1 tablespoon minced garlic
    1 yellow onion, minced
    1-inch piece ginger, peeled and minced
    2 cups peanut butter (natural, creamy style)
    ¼ cup honey
    3 cups boiling water
    1 cup buttermilk
    Green onions, thinly sliced, for garnish

S.O.U.P.S.

1. In a small iron skillet, toast the first seven spices, one at a time, over high heat. Remove each spice from the heat once it begins to change color and the air has a definite spicy odor. Once the spices have cooled sufficiently, mix them and grind them into a fine powder. Set aside.

2. Heat the peanut oil in a stockpot until very hot. With the lid of the stockpot in one hand, pour the brown mustard seeds in the oil and immediately cover. When the popping subsides, remove the lid (it should smell like popcorn).

3. Add the garlic, give the pot a shake, then add the onion and immediately stir to mix. Lower the heat, cover, and let cook for 5 minutes, or until the onion is golden. Add the minced ginger and the ground spices and mix well.

4. Place the peanut butter in a large bowl. Add the honey and whisk until blended. Add the boiling water, 1 cup at a time, whisking after each addition until evenly blended. Pour the contents of the bowl into the pot and mix well. Cover and let the soup reach a boil over medium heat. Stir occasionally so the onions and spices don't burn on the bottom of the pot. Add the buttermilk and stir well. Cover and let simmer for 15 minutes over low heat.

5. Once the soup reaches the consistency of runny pancake batter, remove it from the stove. Serve immediately with thinly sliced green onions.

SUMMER MINESTRONE

2 HOURS PREP TIME • YIELDS TWELVE 1-CUP SERVINGS

Here's a basic minestrone recipe that can be changed with the seasons by simply adding seasonal vegetables. If adding cooked pasta, keep it separate from the soup with a light coating of olive oil, and only add it just before serving. If you plan to use meat, make sure it is properly cooked before adding it.

¼ cup olive oil
1 tablespoon minced garlic
1 small yellow onion, thinly sliced
1 rib celery
1 small carrot, sliced
1 small parsnip, diced
1 small turnip, diced
½ cup red wine, preferably cabernet,
 plus more as needed
1 teaspoon black peppercorns
2 bay leaves
1 tablespoon minced fresh
 thyme leaves
1 tablespoon minced fresh
 oregano leaves

1 tablespoon minced fresh
 rosemary leaves
Kosher salt
4 cups Basic Vegetable Stock
 (page 31)
32-ounce can diced tomatoes,
 strained, half puréed with liquid
2 tablespoons roasted garlic purée
 (page 19) (optional)
¼ pound asparagus, in
 1-inch segments
16-ounce can white beans
16-ounce can kidney beans
Grated parmesan cheese, for garnish

1. Heat the oil in a stockpot over medium-high heat. Add the garlic and sauté until golden. Add the onion. Mix well, cover, and cook until translucent. Add the celery and carrot. Mix well and cover. Cook until slightly tender. Add the parsnip, turnip, wine, peppercorns, bay leaves, thyme, oregano, rosemary, and 1 teaspoon salt. Mix well. Cover and simmer until all the vegetables begin to release their juices, about 20 minutes.

2. Add the stock, diced tomatoes, tomato purée, and the roasted garlic purée, if using. Mix well and cover. Simmer for 20 to 30 minutes.

3. Add the asparagus, the white beans, and kidney beans. Mix well to incorporate. Cover and let simmer for another 20 minutes. Taste and adjust the flavor with additional salt and pepper. Refrigerate the soup overnight before serving.

4. Reheat the soup to a simmer and serve with grated parmesan on top.

COD and TOMATO CHOWDER with ANISE
1½ HOURS PREP TIME • YIELDS TWELVE 1-CUP SERVINGS

Made with fennel bulb and anise seed, this soup is light and fresh with licorice overtones. Use fresh oregano if you cannot find ajawan seeds.

¼ cup unsalted butter
1 tablespoon minced garlic
1 yellow onion, finely chopped
Kosher salt
1 bulb fennel, sliced
12 to 15 medium Roma tomatoes, peeled, seeded, and chopped (page 23), or
   a 32-ounce can diced tomatoes
½ cup white wine
2 bay leaves, crushed
1 teaspoon black peppercorns, coarsely ground
½ teaspoon anise seeds, toasted and crushed
½ teaspoon ajawan seeds, toasted, or 2 tablespoons chopped fresh oregano leaves
2 cups Basic Vegetable Stock (page 31)
2 potatoes, washed and cut into ½-inch cubes
1 pound cod, cut into ½-inch cubes
Sour cream and fresh fennel or dill, for garnish

1. Melt the butter in a stockpot over medium-high heat. Add the garlic, onion, and 1 teaspoon salt. Stir well and cover. Let cook for 5 to 10 minutes.

2. Add the fennel. Stir well and cover. Let cook for 10 more minutes.

3. Add tomatoes, white wine, bay leaves, peppercorns, anise seeds, and ajawan seeds and stir well. Cover and let simmer for another 10 to 15 minutes.

4. Add the stock and potatoes. Stir well, cover, and let cook until the potatoes just begin to become tender—about 30 minutes.

5. Add the cod. Cover and cook until the cod is white and the potatoes are soft—another 10 minutes or so.

6. Remove from the heat and adjust to taste with salt. Garnish with a small dollop of sour cream and a sprig of fennel or fresh dill.

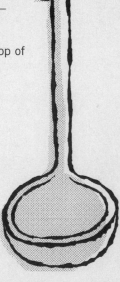

SUMMER

MEDITERRANEAN EGGPLANT SOUP
1 HOUR PREP TIME • YIELDS TEN 1-CUP SERVINGS

When serving this soup I like to garnish it heavily with diced tomatoes, freshly minced parsley, chives, or cilantro and a dash of paprika.

3 medium eggplants
Kosher salt
½ cup tahini (sesame seed paste)
1 head garlic, roasted and puréed (page 19)
¼ cup honey
1 cup yogurt
2 cups water
1/4 cup olive oil
1 large yellow onion, thinly sliced
1 teaspoon cayenne
½ teaspoon turmeric
2 tablespoons lemon juice

1. Preheat the oven to 550°F.

2. Cut the eggplants in half lengthwise. Coat the insides with salt and place on large baking sheet. Bake for 45 minutes.

3. Remove the eggplants from the oven and cool for at least 20 minutes before handling. When cool to the touch, peel away the skins and place the pulp in a food processor bowl. Purée until smooth, adding water if necessary. Strain to remove any seeds. Pour into a stockpot.

4. Purée together the tahini, roasted garlic, honey, yogurt, and enough water to achieve a smooth and runny consistency. Add this to the eggplant purée in the stockpot.

5. Heat the olive oil in a small saucepan. Add the onion, cayenne, turmeric, and 1 teaspoon salt and stir well. Cover and let simmer for about 15 minutes, or until the onion is very soft and mushy. Remove the pot from the heat and purée the onion until smooth. Strain to remove any stringy parts. Add the onion to the eggplant mixture.

6. Place the stockpot over medium-high heat and allow the soup to begin bubbling. When it simmers, turn off the heat, and add the lemon juice. Adjust with salt if necessary. Stir well and serve garnished with diced tomato, freshly minced parsley, cilantro, and chives, or paprika.

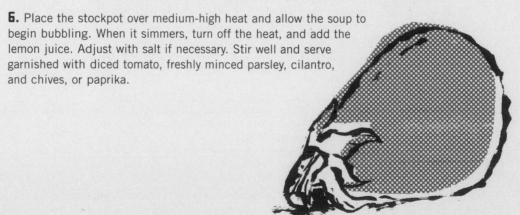

SUMMER

HEARTY MISO SOUP
1 HOUR PREP TIME • YIELDS TEN 1-CUP SERVINGS

If you don't want the heat, replace the sesame chile oil with regular sesame oil and remove the serrano peppers. If you are fond of other ingredients, feel free to add or subtract to your own personal tastes. Just remember, miso is a living culture and boiling the soup will kill it.

¼ cup sesame chile oil
1 yellow onion, sliced
3 cloves garlic, finely sliced
1-inch piece ginger, sliced into thin medallions
2 serrano peppers, thinly sliced
1 shallot, thinly sliced
1 pound firm tofu, in small cubes
¼ pound shiitake mushroom caps, thinly sliced
4 tablespoons red miso
4 cups hot water
¼ cup soy sauce
¼ cup tahini (sesame seed paste)
3 leaves kale, stems removed, cut into strips
Green onions and toasted sesame seeds, for garnish

1. Heat the sesame chile oil in a soup pot. Add the onion and sauté until tender. Add the garlic, ginger, and serrano peppers and stir well. Cover and cook for 5 minutes. Add the shallot, tofu, and mushrooms and mix well. Cover and cook for another 5 minutes.

2. Mix the miso with the hot water. Stir in the soy sauce and tahini. Add this mixture to the soup pot. Drop in the kale. Stir well and cover. Reduce the heat to medium and let simmer for about 15 minutes. Do not let the soup reach a boil.

3. Remove the soup from the heat. Garnish with thinly sliced green onions and toasted sesame seeds and serve right away.

SUMMER

GAZPACHO
1 TO 1½ HOURS PREP TIME • YIELDS FOUR TO EIGHT 1-CUP SERVINGS

This soup is a mystery to me. It is widely popular in the South; however, in the North people seem to be a little weary when it comes to cold soups. Though not your typical Seattle soup, it is quite refreshing and light. There are many ways to make this soup. This specific version is the one I prefer as I find the vegetables much more intense after they have been roasted.

2 pounds ripe Roma tomatoes, cut in
  half lengthwise
1 medium eggplant, peeled and cut
  into 1½-inch cubes
1 yellow onion, coarsely chopped
3 jalapeño peppers, quartered
  and seeded
1 medium shallot, minced
1 tablespoon sugar
1 tablespoon kosher salt
1 tablespoon cracked
  black peppercorns
1 cup olive oil

1 head garlic, roasted (page 19)
1 cup red wine, preferably Spanish,
  such as Rioja
1 tablespoon minced fresh oregano
1 tablespoon minced fresh thyme
1 tablespoon minced fresh rosemary
2 tablespoons balsamic vinegar
4 cups Basic Vegetable Stock
  (page 31)
Minced cilantro and sour cream or
crème fraîche, for garnish
Cuban bread or a baguette, for serving

1. Preheat the oven to 450°F.

2. Toss together the tomatoes, eggplant, onion, jalapeños, shallot, sugar, salt, peppercorns, and olive oil in a roasting pan. Roast for 45 minutes, removing the pan from the oven every 15 minutes and stirring the vegetables around. Make sure that they are well coated with the oil and not sticking to the pan or burning. When the tomato skins have shriveled and the eggplant is very tender, almost mushy, turn off the oven and remove the pan. Set it aside and allow the vegetables to cool until they are easy to handle.

3. In a food processor, purée the roasted garlic and the roasted vegetables in batches. Strain through a sieve or press through a wire mesh strainer. Discard any seeds or skins that are left behind in the strainer. When all of the vegetables are out of the roasting pan and you are about to purée the last batch of them, whisk the wine around in the roasting pan to pick up any caramelized bits and pieces that may have stuck to the pan and add this to the food processor. Purée the last batch and strain.

4. Add the fresh herbs, balsamic vinegar, and vegetable stock to the soup. Whisk well and chill overnight, giving time for the flavors to marry.

5. Serve the soup with a garnish of minced cilantro and a small dollop of sour cream or a spoonful of crème fraîche. If you can find Cuban bread, serve it with this soup. If not, a crusty baguette will do just as well.

COLD STRAWBERRY SOUP
30 MINUTES PREP TIME • YIELDS FOUR TO EIGHT 1-CUP SERVINGS

I'm a strawberry fiend. I adore fresh, tender, juicy, sweet, blood red strawberries. There is nothing quite like them. I admit it; I am a strawberry junkie. I first made this soup back in Albuquerque as an option for desert. I was quite surprised to see people ordering it as a regular soup with their meals.

2 quarts very ripe strawberries, hulled and washed
1 cup port
1 cup sour cream
1 cup heavy cream
1 cup sugar
Grated zest of 1 orange
1 teaspoon cracked black peppercorns (optional)
Thinly sliced fresh mint leaves or whole sprigs, for garnish

1. Purée the strawberries, in batches, in a food processor until smooth. Press the puréed pulp through a strainer into a large bowl. Discard any seeds or bits of flesh that remain in the strainer. Repeat this process until all the strawberries are puréed and strained.

2. Add the port, sour cream, heavy cream, sugar, and orange zest and whisk all the ingredients together until the soup's texture is even and the color is rosy pink. Taste and adjust with sugar, port, or sour cream to reach the flavor and consistency you prefer. Add the black peppercorns if you wish. They add depth to the soup and give it a bit of bite.

3. Ladle into soup bowls, garnish with mint, and serve.

A thin, brothy, and light soup with a delightfully fragrant flavor, this is perfect for the summer months. If you do not care for the spiciness, just omit the peppers or cayenne.

1½ cups red lentils, picked over and washed
¼ teaspoon turmeric
1 pound ripe tomatoes, peeled, or 16-ounce can diced tomatoes
2 tablespoons tamarind paste, diluted in 1 cup water, or 1 tablespoon lemon juice
1½ teaspoons cumin seeds, toasted and ground
2 teaspoons coriander seeds, toasted and ground
½ yellow onion, finely chopped
½ teaspoon cayenne, or 2 to 4 jalapeño, serrano, or Thai peppers, finely chopped
2 teaspoons kosher salt
2 tablespoons minced fresh garlic
1 teaspoon black mustard seeds
⅛ teaspoon asafetida
12 curry leaves, or 2 tablespoons chopped fresh cilantro leaves
1 tablespoon ghee
Chopped fresh cilantro, for garnish

1. Heat 8 cups of water in a soup pot to a boil. Add the lentils and the turmeric, stirring well to keep the lentils from clumping. Cover, leaving the lid ajar, and cook the lentils until done, 20 to 45 minutes. The lentils are done when they are extremely tender but not mushy. Remove from the heat and strain. Discard the water and set the lentils aside. Clean the pot.

SUMMER

2. Mince or purée the pulp of the tomatoes. Coarsely dice the tomato skins and set both aside.

3. Pour the lentils and 1 cup of water into the cleaned soup pot. Using a whisk, break up the lentils. Add the tamarind paste, if using, to the lentils and water, whisking it well into the mixture. Add the minced tomatoes, cumin, coriander, onion, cayenne, if using, and salt. Bring to a boil over medium-high heat. Lower the heat, stir well, partially cover, and allow to simmer for about 10 to 15 minutes.

4. Remove the pot from the heat and add the diced tomatoes and the lemon juice, if using. Stir well and set aside.

5. Have the garlic, mustard seeds, asafetida, peppers, if using, and curry leaves in small separate piles next to the stove. Heat the ghee in a saucepan over high heat until it begins to change color. Add the mustard seeds to the ghee and cover quickly with the lid to keep the mustard seeds from spattering all over the kitchen.

6. Once the seeds have stopped spattering and you get a cooked popcorn smell, add the asafetida. Give the pan a quick shake and then add the garlic and peppers. Sauté until the garlic turns golden or light brown and the skin of the peppers begins to blister. Carefully add the curry leaves. (Warning: They make a lot of noise when coming into contact with the hot oil.) Using tongs or a long spoon, stir the leaves so that they are evenly fried.

7. Remove the infused ghee from the heat and carefully pour it over the soup. Be careful—the oil might spatter upon contact with the water in the soup. Stir well and serve. If you are using the chopped cilantro, now is the time to add it to the soup.

One summer I decided to try to roast vegetables before using them in soup. I know that tomatoes and eggplant complement each other so I decided to try something radically different than the Mediterranean Eggplant Soup (page 90). The eggplant is roasted and left in nice healthy pieces.

- 1 medium eggplant, peeled and cut into ½-inch cubes
- 1 pound Roma tomatoes, cut in half and seeded
- 1 yellow onion, coarsely chopped
- 1 tablespoon capers
- ¼ cup olive oil
- ¼ cup balsamic vinegar
- 1 tablespoon cracked black peppercorns
- 1 tablespoon chopped fresh rosemary
- 2 tablespoons minced fresh thyme
- 1 tablespoon chopped fresh oregano
- 8 cups Basic Vegetable Stock (page 31)
- 1 head garlic, roasted and puréed (page 19)
- 1 tablespoon kosher salt
- ¼ cup white wine
- ¼ cup thinly sliced fresh basil
- Croutons or a crusty baguette, for serving

SUMMER

1. Preheat the oven to 450°F.

2. Place the eggplant, tomatoes, onion, capers, olive oil, balsamic vinegar, peppercorns, rosemary, thyme, and oregano in a bowl and mix well. Make sure that everything is glazed with a nice coat of the liquid. Pour into a roasting pan and place in the oven. Check every 15 minutes, stirring to make sure that nothing is sticking to the pan. When the eggplant is tender, 30 to 45 minutes, turn off the oven and remove the pan. Set aside.

3. Heat the stock and the garlic purée in a soup pot over medium heat. Add the roasted vegetables and salt. Stir well and allow to simmer over low heat for a few minutes. Pour the wine into the roasting pan and whisk it around to pick up any of the remaining herbs and particles. Pour this into the soup pot and stir again to mix well.

4. Remove the soup from the heat and stir in the basil leaves. Serve immediately with croutons or a crusty baguette.

This refreshingly light late summer/early fall soup is one that I dared to try at the Hopvine with a worried anticipation that it might not be well received. The soup was quite the hit. I was quite pleased at its sweet and subtle aroma and its beautiful coloring. One bit of warning though: Try not to reheat this soup. Every time it is reheated the squid cooks a bit more, which can lead to that notoriously rubbery texture.

¼ teaspoon saffron threads, crumbled
½ cup boiling water
¼ cup peanut oil
1 teaspoon brown mustard seeds
8 Thai peppers, cut into
   ¼-inch segments
2 tablespoons minced garlic
1 yellow onion, thinly sliced
2 shallots, minced
1-inch piece ginger, peeled
   and minced

6 Roma tomatoes, peeled, halved,
   seeded, and chopped, or 14-ounce
   can diced tomatoes, drained
4 cups Basic Vegetable Stock
   (page 31) or Basic Fish Stock
   (page 29)
1 tablespoon kosher salt
14-ounce can coconut milk
1 pound small squid, cut into squares,
   tentacles left whole
2 tablespoons coarsely
   chopped cilantro

1. Add the saffron to the boiling water and set aside.

2. Heat the oil in a soup pot. When it begins to smoke, add the mustard seeds and quickly cover the pot with the lid ajar. When the aroma of popcorn is noticeable, and/or the mustard

SUMMER

seeds have stopped popping, add the chopped peppers and quickly sauté them, stirring, until the skins begin to blister. Add the garlic and sauté until it turns golden. Add the onion and shallots. Stir well, cover, and cook until the onions become translucent and tender.

3. Add the ginger, stir well, and sauté for 5 minutes. Add the tomatoes, stock, salt, coconut milk and the saffron-infused water. Stir well, cover, and allow it to reach a boil. Lower the heat to medium and add the squid. Stir well, cover, and allow the soup to simmer for 10 minutes. Taste the squid to check its tenderness: You do not want chewy squid; you want tender squid. The flesh should turn opaque white and have a glistening sheen to it. If the squid has not reached the proper consistency, continue to simmer for another 5 minutes and check again. Repeat until the squid is just cooked through.

4. Remove the soup from the heat. Stir in the cilantro and serve immediately.

Whenever I make a meat-based soup at the Hopvine, I immediately try it out vegetarian style; that way I can get a better read from the customers as to whether or not the soup is a success. This stew is much like Lamb Vindaloo (page 105). The best way to get the flavor to come out of the vegetables is to roast them in the oven before adding them to the pot. This is a spicy summer stew, so warn your guests.

1 pound new red potatoes, washed and cubed into bite-size pieces

½ head cauliflower, chopped into bite-size florets

1 small eggplant, cubed into bite-size pieces

½ cup peanut oil

2 yellow onions, chopped

1-inch piece of ginger, peeled

6 garlic cloves

10 to 20 Thai, jalapeño, or serrano peppers, stems removed, half chopped and set in a separate pile

2 tablespoons curry powder

¼ cup distilled vinegar

1 teaspoon brown mustard seeds

1 cup water

1 cup fresh or frozen peas

¼ cup lemon juice

2 cups yogurt

2 tablespoons coarsely chopped cilantro

1 tablespoon kosher salt (optional)

1. Preheat the oven to 450°F.

2. Toss the potatoes, cauliflower, and eggplant in a roasting pan with ¼ cup of the peanut

SUMMER

oil. Coat the vegetables well. Roast, stirring occasionally, for about 30 minutes, or until the cauliflower begins to crisp, and the potato skins begin to shrivel and their flesh begins to turn golden brown. Remove the roasting pan and set aside.

3. Put the onions, ginger, garlic, 5 to 10 whole peppers, curry powder, and vinegar in a food processor and purée until wet and evenly mixed. Remove from the food processor and set aside.

4. Heat the remaining ¼ cup of oil in a soup pot over high heat. Add the mustard seeds and cover quickly, leaving the lid ajar. When the popping subsides and the mustard seeds give off an aroma akin to fresh popcorn, add the chopped peppers. Fry them until the skins shrivel and begin to change color. Add the onion and curry purée to the oil and stir well. Cover the pot and allow the paste to fry.

5. When the onion paste begins to give off a strong curry aroma, add the water and all the roasted vegetables. Stir well to coat everything evenly, cover the pot, and lower the heat to medium. If the potatoes are not tender enough to eat, the cauliflower is still too raw, or the eggplant is still too firm, simmer the stew for about 20 minutes, or until the potatoes are easily pierced with a fork, the cauliflower is tender to the bite, and the eggplant is soft to the touch. Do not let any of the vegetables get completely cooked or mushy, otherwise the stew will become extremely pasty as the starches begin to break down.

6. Add the peas, lemon juice, yogurt, and the cilantro. Stir well and taste. If you feel that the soup needs salt, add it at this time. Otherwise you may omit it from the soup. Remove from the heat and serve.

Everybody at the pub is used to the vegetarian options I tend to offer, so I decided to shock some of the customers by working with lamb. This stew was my offering to the world of red meat. Those who were inclined to eat it more or less inhaled their servings. It just goes to show that a good hot and spicy soup can be enjoyed in the summer. If you wish, this stew can be served side by side with a steaming pile of basmati rice instead of bread.

2 yellow onions, coarsely chopped
1-inch piece of ginger, peeled
6 garlic cloves
2 tablespoons curry powder
¼ cup distilled vinegar
5 to 15 jalapeño, serrano, or Thai peppers, stems removed, half chopped
   and set in a separate pile
1 cup peanut oil, plus more if needed
1 pound new potatoes, washed and diced
1 pound lamb, trimmed of fat and cubed
1 teaspoon brown mustard seeds
1 tablespoon kosher salt
1 cup water
¼ cup lemon juice
2 cups yogurt, plus more for garnish

1. Place the onions, ginger, garlic, curry powder, vinegar, the whole peppers, and a little water in the food processor. Purée into a smooth and watery paste.

2. Heat the oil in a soup pot. Add the potatoes and fry until golden on the edges and the skin begins to shrivel. Remove the potatoes from the oil and set aside on paper towels to soak up any excess oil.

3. Let oil get hot again, then add the lamb. Brown the edges of the lamb. Remove from the oil and set aside with the potatoes.

4. Allow the oil to get smoking hot. If most of the oil has been soaked up by the potatoes and lamb, add another ¼ cup of peanut oil to the pot. Add the mustard seeds and cover the pot partially with a lid until the seeds stop popping and an aroma similar to popcorn rises. Add the chopped peppers. Sauté until the edges look blistered.

5. Pour the puréed onion mixture into the oil and stir well. Lower the heat to medium and let the paste simmer in the oil for about 15 to 20 minutes, or until you smell a very strong scent of onions, curry, garlic, and ginger. Let your nose decide when it is time to proceed to the next step.

6. Add the potatoes, lamb, salt, and water. Stir well, cover, and allow to simmer until the potatoes are cooked through.

7. Remove from the heat and add the lemon juice and yogurt to the soup. Stir well. Serve with an extra dollop of yogurt.

AUTUMN

CELERY and ROQUEFORT SOUP
1 HOUR PREP TIME • YIELDS EIGHT 1-CUP SERVINGS

Surprisingly strong and pungent, this soup should be served only to people who truly enjoy Roquefort. Crumble more cheese on top or serve with celery ribs and minced parsley. I also suggest slivered almonds to add crunch and a subtle nutty flavor to the soup.

> ¼ cup unsalted butter
> 1 yellow onion, sliced
> 1 bunch celery, finely sliced, including leaves
> Kosher salt
> ¾ cup Roquefort or blue cheese
> 1 cup milk
> ½ bunch parsley stems and leaves, coarsely chopped
> ½ cup dry white wine
> Black peppercorns, cracked
> 4 cups Basic Vegetable Stock (page 31)
> 1 cup cream
> 1 teaspoon celery seeds

1. Melt the butter in a soup pot over high heat without browning. Add the onion and celery with 1 teaspoon salt. Mix well, lower the heat to medium, cover, and let simmer until reduced at least by half, 20 to 30 minutes.

2. Meanwhile, purée the cheese and the milk in the food processor until smooth. If necessary, scrape down the sides of the bowl with a spatula to incorporate pieces of cheese. Set aside.

3. Once the onion and celery have reduced, add the parsley, wine, peppercorns, and the stock and mix well. Cover and let simmer for 5 to 10 minutes, or until the liquid is hot.

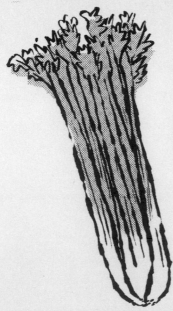

4. Remove the pot from the heat. Purée and strain the contents. Discard anything that remains at the bottom of the strainer. Thoroughly clean out the pot.

5. Return the purée to the pot. Add the cheese purée, the cream, and the celery seeds. Cover and let simmer for about 10 minutes. The soup's color should be a very pale green.

6. Remove from the heat. Top the soup with slivered almonds before serving or use celery stalks, crumbled cheese, and minced parsley.

HUBBARD SQUASH SOUP with BACON and PINEAPPLE
2½ HOURS PREP TIME • YIELDS TEN 1-CUP SERVINGS

Hubbard squash is available in the fall—the same time as the mighty pumpkin. However, this gourd seems to have a longer season (perhaps because not so many children are clamoring to carve them up) and continues to appear in markets until early to middle winter.

> **Olive oil**
> **1 small Hubbard squash**
> **Kosher salt**
> **½ pound bacon, plus more for garnish**
> **1 tablespoon minced garlic**
> **1 yellow onion, diced**
> **14-ounce can crushed pineapple**
> **1 tablespoon fresh thyme, leaves only**
> **1 teaspoon black peppercorns, cracked**
> **½ cup pure maple syrup, plus more for garnish**
> **4 cups Basic Vegetable Stock (page 31)**

1. Preheat the oven to 500°F. Coat a rimmed baking sheet with a light layer of olive oil.

2. Cut the squash in half and remove the seeds and strings. Cover the flesh of the squash with a thin layer of salt. Place the squash on the baking sheet, cut side down. Bake for about 1 hour, or until the flesh is tender and falling from the skin.

3. Meanwhile, cook the bacon, saving the drippings for the soup. When cool, crumble the bacon. Pour all the bacon fat into the soup pot.

4. Add the garlic and sauté over high heat until golden brown. Add the onion and 1 teaspoon salt. Stir, cover, and cook until tender. Add the pineapple, including its juice, and the thyme. Mix well and cover. Reduce the heat to medium and simmer until the flavors are well combined, about 5 minutes. Add the peppercorns and the maple syrup. Stir well and let simmer for about 10 minutes.

5. When the squash is cool enough to handle, scrape the flesh away from the skin and place in a food processor. Purée until smooth, adding a little stock if necessary. Do this in batches until all the squash is puréed. Add the squash purée and the rest of the stock to the soup pot and mix well. Add the crumbled bacon and stir well. Cover and let simmer until the soup just starts to boil. Remove from the heat and adjust to taste with additional salt and cracked black pepper.

6. Serve with a sprinkling of bacon and a drizzle of maple syrup.

AUTUMN

CABBAGE and APPLE SOUP with JUNIPER BERRIES

1½ HOURS PREP TIME • YIELDS TEN 1-CUP SERVINGS

Both cabbage and apples come into season in autumn, which is a perfect time to eat this rich and delicious cream soup. The soup can be carried through the winter months by using the different varieties of apples that ripen throughout the season.

4 tablespoons unsalted butter
1½ yellow onions, thinly sliced
2 tablespoons white wine vinegar
2 apples, such as Fuji, Cameo, or Braeburn, sliced
Kosher salt
1 teaspoon white peppercorns, ground
1 tablespoon juniper berries, crushed
1 cup hard apple cider
1 small head green cabbage, cored and shredded
4 cups Basic Vegetable Stock (page 31)
2 cups cream

1. Melt 2 tablespoons of the butter in a soup pot. Add the onions and stir well. Cover and let cook for about 10 to 15 minutes, stirring occasionally to make sure the onions don't burn. Once the onions begin to caramelize, add the vinegar. Stir the onions well to help glaze them with the vinegar. Let cook for about 3 to 5 minutes, or until the vinegar evaporates. Remove the onions from the soup pot and set aside.

2. Without cleaning the pot, return it to the heat and melt the remaining 2 tablespoons butter. Add the apple slices and 1 teaspoon salt. Stir well and cover. Let simmer for 10 minutes, or until the juice from the apples is released. Add the peppercorns, juniper berries, and cider. Mix well and cover. Let simmer for about 10 minutes.

3. Add another teaspoon of salt. Slowly incorporate the shredded cabbage to the pot. Add a little at a time, mix well, cover, and allow to simmer for a couple of minutes. Repeat the additions of cabbage until it all fits into the pot.

4. Once all the cabbage is in the pot, add the caramelized onions and the stock. Mix well, cover, and let cook for about 15 minutes.

5. Add the cream and mix well. Cover and allow to reach a simmer. Remove from the heat and adjust taste with salt and white pepper. Chill for 1 day to meld the flavors.

6. To serve, heat the soup to a simmer but not to a boil.

This soup can be made year round since mushrooms are easy to acquire. Since this soup uses cream, I suggest making it in the autumn and winter months.

1 large baking potato
6 tablespoons unsalted butter
1 shallot, thinly sliced
1 yellow onion, thinly sliced
¼ cup cream sherry
2 pounds mushrooms, cremini, white button, or a mix, finely sliced and half the caps set aside

4 cups Basic Vegetable Stock (page 31)
Black peppercorns
Kosher salt
2 to 4 bay leaves, crumbled
2 cups cream
1 tablespoon minced fresh thyme

1. Preheat the oven to 550°F.

2. Cook the potato until a fork or knife can be easily inserted, about 30 to 45 minutes. Set aside to cool.

3. Melt 4 tablespoons of the butter in a soup pot. Add the shallot and onion. Stir well and cover. Cook for 10 minutes, or until they begin to caramelize. Add the sherry and stir to pick up any caramelized bits that have stuck to the bottom of the pot.

4. Add the sliced mushrooms, saving half of the caps for later. Mix and cover for a few minutes to extract the liquid from the mushrooms and for the mushrooms to reduce in size.

5. Add about 2 cups of the stock, along with 1 teaspoon peppercorns, 1 teaspoon salt, and the bay leaves. Mix well and cover. Let the soup simmer for about 30 minutes, or until everything is very soft.

6. Meanwhile, scoop out the flesh of the potato and purée it in a food processor. Add the rest of the stock to help the potato gain a smooth and creamy consistency. Set aside.

7. In batches, purée the mushroom, onion, and shallot mixture. Press each batch through a strainer over a storage container. Discard anything that remains at the bottom of the strainer Clean the pot.

8. Whisk the potato purée and the cream into the mushrooms. Set aside.

9. Melt the remaining 2 tablespoons of butter in the pot. When completely melted, add the reserved mushroom caps, 1 teaspoon salt, and the thyme and mix well. Cover and let cook until reduced. If you remove the lid and you are greeted with a wonderful aroma of mushrooms, you know they are ready.

10. Add the soup and mix well. Let simmer until it thickens slightly. Adjust to taste with salt and cracked peppercorns.

11. Chill for a day to meld the flavors.

12. Reheat to a simmer before serving.

SOUTHWESTERN PUMPKIN SOUP

20 MINUTES PREP TIME • YIELDS TEN 1-CUP SERVINGS

This soup is sooooo simple to make. Obviously you can serve this soup all year round even though pumpkin harvest is in the early autumn. Apparently, the canned pumpkin tree is quite prolific and can produce large quantities of canned pumpkin any month of the year.

¼ teaspoon cloves
2 teaspoons coriander seeds
2 teaspoons cumin seeds
½ teaspoon black peppercorns
2 teaspoons red chile powder
1 teaspoon ground cinnamon
1 teaspoon garlic powder
¼ teaspoon freshly ground nutmeg
4 cups Basic Vegetable Stock
   (page 31)

2 cups cream
32-ounce can pumpkin purée
½ cup pure maple syrup
Kosher salt
Grated cheddar cheese, toasted
   walnuts, and minced fresh cilantro,
   for garnish

1. Toast the cloves, coriander seeds, cumin seeds, and peppercorns in a small hot skillet. Let cool and grind together to a powder. Blend with the red chile powder, cinnamon, garlic powder, and nutmeg. Set aside.

2. Pour the stock and the cream into a soup pot over medium-high heat. Cover and heat until steaming.

3. Meanwhile, put the pumpkin in a large mixing bowl. Add the maple syrup, 1 teaspoon salt, and the combined spices. Whisk well to incorporate all the flavors.

4. When the stock and cream are simmering, slowly add a little of the pumpkin mixture. Whisk to break it up. Add a little more. Repeat until all of the pumpkin is in the pot. Cover and let simmer until the soup thickens.

5. Garnish with grated cheddar cheese, toasted walnuts, and cilantro.

POTATO-LEEK SOUP
1½ HOURS PREP TIME • YIELDS TEN 1-CUP SERVINGS

Always a popular soup, this one fits the term "comfort food." You will always be the belle of the ball when you serve this soup. If the basic recipe seems pretty bland and boring, jazz it up. Add herbs, such as rosemary, thyme, or oregano, with the leeks in the beginning. Add harder vegetables (carrots and fennel bulbs) when you add the potatoes. Softer vegetables (celery and mushrooms) go in about 20 minutes after the potatoes. Other good additions are roasted garlic purée (page 19) and cubed cooked chicken breast.

¼ cup unsalted butter
3 leeks, washed and thinly sliced
½ cup flour
2½ cups hot water
½ cup cream sherry
2 large potatoes, peeled, thinly sliced, and soaking in cold water
Kosher salt
2 teaspoons black peppercorns, cracked
1 cup cream
2 cups milk
Green onions and butter, for garnish

1. Melt the butter in a soup pot. Add the leeks and stir well. Cover the pot and cook until leeks reduce in size and are very tender. Remove from the heat and let cool for about 5 minutes.

2. Add the flour and mix well to incorporate the flour with the butter. Add the hot water and sherry and whisk well to remove any lumps. Add the potatoes and 1 tablespoon salt and mix well. Return the pot to medium heat and cover. Let cook until the potato slices are tender.

3. Add the peppercorns, cream, and milk to the soup. Mix well, reduce the heat to low, and cover. Let the soup cook until it thickens slightly. Be careful with this soup. It can scorch and leave a burnt flavor. Keep the heat lower than you would normally. If you feel something sticking to the bottom of the pan, reduce the heat and gently ease the items up. If you find any burnt pieces while stirring the soup, pick them out and discard them. Remove from the heat and adjust the seasoning to taste.

4. Serve with chopped green onions and a pat of butter.

THAI CHICKEN SOUP with PAPAYA and DUMPLINGS
2 DAYS FOR STOCK; 1½ HOURS TO FINISH SOUP • YIELDS TEN 1-CUP SERVINGS

This recipe is my tribute to fusion cuisine—chicken and dumplings with a Thai twist. This soup can be extremely hot. If you want it milder, adjust the number of the chilies. The stock takes roughly 2 days to make, but it's worth it. Make in late fall and early winter when papayas are in season.

STOCK
6 quarts (24 cups) Basic Chicken Stock (page 33)
2 whole chickens, chopped into 3-inch pieces, breast meat reserved
2 yellow onions, unpeeled and coarsely chopped
3- to 4-inch piece of ginger, coarsely chopped
1 stalk lemongrass, coarsely chopped
2 tablespoons coriander seeds
3 tablespoons kosher salt
8 to 10 dried red chilies, broken in half and seeds shaken out
10 lime leaves (optional)
8 pieces dried galangal root (optional)
3-inch cinnamon stick broken into pieces
2 heads garlic, unpeeled and broken up

DUMPLINGS

1 cup flour
2 tablespoons chicken fat,
   from the stock
Pinch kosher salt
Pinch cayenne
1 teaspoon minced garlic
1 teaspoon minced ginger
2 eggs

RAFT

12 egg whites, whisked
12 egg shells, cleaned and crushed
2 yellow onions, minced
3-inch piece ginger, peeled and
   minced
2 carrots, minced

SOUP

1 tablespoon coconut oil
1 yellow onion, thinly sliced
2 to 4 serrano or Thai peppers,
   thinly sliced
¼ stalk lemongrass, finely sliced
   or minced
2 chicken breasts, cut into
   ½-inch cubes
1 ripe papaya, peeled, seeded, and
   cut into ½-inch cubes
4 cups stock (page 120)
14-ounce can coconut milk

1. For the stock, place all the stock items, except the chicken breasts, in a stockpot filled with cold water. Cover and let reach a boil. Reduce the heat to medium-low and let simmer for at least 8 hours.

2. Remove from heat and strain through a colander. Dispose of anything left in the colander.

AUTUMN

3. Leave uncovered and chill overnight in the refrigerator. When completely cold, skim the layer of fat from the top and set aside. You will use this congealed fat in the dumplings.

4. For the dumplings, combine all the dumpling ingredients. The result will resemble a thick and very sticky paste. Let sit for 20 minutes.

5. Return the stock to a boil.

6. With a spoon, quickly add 1-inch diameter pieces of the dumpling mixture to the boiling stock.

7. Remove dumplings from the stock as they float to the top of the pot. Set aside.

8. For the raft, put the defatted stock back onto the stove, cover, and let it reach a boil. Be careful it doesn't overflow.

9. Whisk together all the raft ingredients in a large bowl and set aside. Once the stock boils, slide the contents of the bowl onto the top of the stock. Do not stir. Cover the stockpot again. Once it reaches a second boil, turn the heat down to medium-low or low. Let simmer for about 1 hour.

10. Remove the lid and slowly and carefully remove the raft of egg whites, shells, and vegetables from the stock. Place two layers of cheesecloth in a strainer and place the strainer over a storage container. Slowly pour the stock through the strainer. Discard any particles left in the cheesecloth.

11. Heat the coconut oil in a stockpot. Add the onion and sauté until tender and slightly translucent. Add the peppers and lemongrass. Stir well, cover, and let cook for 10 minutes.

12. Add the chicken, stir well, and cover. Cook until the chicken turns completely white on the outside. It isn't necessary at this point for the chicken to be cooked all the way through.

13. Add the papaya, stock, and coconut milk. Mix well, cover, and let simmer until the chicken is cooked all the way through.

14. To serve, ladle the simmering soup into bowls with enough room left for the dumplings, then place however many dumplings you wish in the soup.

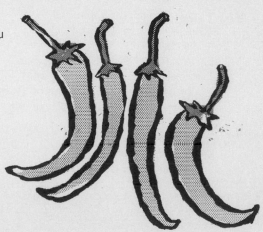

AUTUMN

CREAM OF CAULIFLOWER SOUP WITH ALMONDS
1½ HOURS PREP TIME • YIELDS TEN 1-CUP SERVINGS

This light and refreshing soup is perfect for fall when cauliflower is in season. The lemon zest heightens the flavor and the almonds are a subtle addition. If you want to omit the nutmeg, feel free to do so. When prepping the cauliflower, include the leaves; just remove any discolored or brown spots.

¼ cup unsalted butter
1 tablespoon minced garlic
1 yellow onion, thinly sliced
Kosher salt
½ cup blanched almonds, finely ground
1 teaspoon white peppercorns, ground
4 cups Basic Vegetable Stock (page 31) or Basic Chicken Stock (page 33)
2 pounds cauliflower, stalks minced, half the florets reserved
2 cups cream
¼ cup cream sherry
Grated zest of ½ lemon
Grated nutmeg, for garnish

1. Melt the butter in a soup pot over medium-high heat. Add the garlic and sauté until golden. Add the onion and 1 teaspoon salt. Stir well, cover, and cook until the onion is translucent.

2. Add the almonds, peppercorns, and stock. Stir well and cover. Let simmer for 10 minutes, or until the stock begins to boil. Stir occasionally to keep the almonds from burning at the bottom of the pot.

3. Separate the cauliflower into 2 piles: a larger pile of the stalks and half the florets, and a smaller pile of the rest of the florets. Finely slice the stalks and florets in the larger pile. Coarsely chop the smaller pile, just to break up some of the larger pieces into bite-size morsels. Put the larger pile into the soup pot. Add another teaspoon salt. Mix well, lower the heat to medium, cover, and cook until the cauliflower is very soft. Stir occasionally to keep the almonds from burning.

4. Purée in batches and strain each batch into a storage container. Discard anything that remains in the strainer.

5. Wash out the pot. Place the puréed soup back into it along with the cream, sherry, and the second batch of florets. Stir well. Cover and let simmer over medium-low heat until heated completely through and the cauliflower is cooked. Add the lemon zest. Stir well and remove from the heat.

6. Serve immediately with freshly grated nutmeg.

BUTTERNUT SQUASH SOUP WITH PEARS AND CRANBERRIES

This is a great fall soup. Cranberries, pears, and butternut squash are all in season. The soup is rich but not as hearty as you might expect. If you want to garnish it, I would suggest a slice of fresh pear on top.

- 2 pounds butternut squash
- 4 tablespoons unsalted butter
- 1½ yellow onions, finely sliced
- Kosher salt
- 4 cups Basic Vegetable Stock (page 31) or Basic Chicken Stock (page 33)
- 1 teaspoon white peppercorns, ground
- 3 ripe pears, peeled, cored, and diced, some slices reserved for garnish
- ¼ pound cranberries
- ¾ cup pear cider

1. Preheat the oven to 500°F.

2. Cut the squash in half and remove the seeds and strings. Place the squash on the baking sheet, cut side down. Roast the squash for 40 minutes to 1 hour, or until soft. Let cool. When cool enough to handle, scrape the flesh from the skins. Set aside.

3. Melt 2 tablespoons of the butter in a soup pot over medium-high heat. Add the onions and 1 teaspoon salt. Stir well and cover. Cook until the onion is very soft.

4. Add the squash, stock, white peppercorns, and another teaspoon salt and stir well. Cover and let simmer for 15 minutes, stirring occasionally to keep the soup from burning at the bottom of the pot.

5. Purée the soup in batches, press through a strainer, keep in a storage container and set aside. Discard anything that remains in the strainer. Clean out the pot.

6. Add the remaining 2 tablespoons of butter to the pot, melt over medium-high heat, and add the diced pears and cranberries. Stir well, cover, and let cook for 20 minutes, or until the cranberries are soft but not mushy.

7. Add the pear cider. Stir well and cover. Simmer until the contents have a thick glaze on them, about 10 minutes.

8. Pour the soup back into the pot. Heat through and serve immediately with a fresh pear slice on top.

FUJI APPLE and GORGONZOLA SOUP
1½ HOURS PREP TIME • YIELDS TEN 1-CUP SERVINGS

This soup is similar to the Celery and Roquefort Soup (page 108). I ended up creating it because a certain cheese didn't show up at the pub, so I worked with what I had. Curiously, I like this soup more than the Celery and Roquefort. That, however, is one man's opinion.

¼ cup unsalted butter
1 yellow onion, finely sliced
3 ribs celery, finely sliced
½ cup crumbled gorgonzola cheese
4 cups Basic Vegetable Stock (page 31)
2 Fuji apples, cored, peeled, and finely sliced
¼ bunch parsley, coarsely chopped
Kosher salt
White peppercorns, ground
2 bay leaves, crumbled
½ cup white wine
2 cups milk
¼ teaspoon celery seeds
Grated nutmeg, toasted walnuts, and grated Fuji apple, for garnish

1. Melt the butter in a soup pot over medium-high heat. Add the onion and celery and stir until well coated with the butter. Cover and let cook until the onion is translucent.

2. Meanwhile, purée the gorgonzola in the food processor while slowly adding 2 cups of the stock. Stop the processor occasionally to scrape down the sides of the bowl. Place in a bowl and set aside. Clean out the processor.

3. Once the onions have become translucent, add the apples, parsley, 1 teaspoon salt, 1 teaspoon peppercorns, and bay leaves. Mix well, cover, and let simmer until the apples become soft.

4. Add the wine. Reduce the heat to medium and stir well. Cover and cook for another 15 to 20 minutes.

5. In batches, purée the contents of the soup pot. Press each batch through a strainer into a storage container. Discard anything that remains in the strainer.

6. Clean out the pot, put back on the stove, and keep the heat at medium. Add the puréed vegetables, the puréed cheese, the rest of the stock, and the milk. Whisk until evenly blended. Whisk in the celery seeds.

7. Cover and allow the soup to heat through, about 10 minutes. Adjust to taste with salt, wine, or peppercorns. Add stock if the soup seems too thick.

8. Ladle the soup into bowls and garnish with grated nutmeg, toasted walnuts, and/or grated Fuji apple.

CHICKEN BROTH WITH CREMINI AND PASTA
30 TO 45 MINUTES PREP TIME • YIELDS SIX 1-CUP SERVINGS

I had been trying to come up with a few different ways to work with chicken stock. While talking to my mother, she suggested a simple broth with a few vegetables—something comforting yet light. I thought about this "radical" experiment in simplicity and came up with a soup that is perfect for Seattle's chilly autumn nights. The tender sautéed mushrooms and the thinly sliced green onions fit perfectly with the al dente pasta shells. Thanks, Mom, for the inspiration!

¼ cup chicken fat or olive oil
1 pound cremini mushrooms, cleaned, stems removed, and sliced about ⅛ inch thick
4 green onions, thinly sliced on the diagonal

8 cups clarified chicken stock (page 37)
Kosher salt
2 cups shell pasta or other small pasta
2 tablespoons olive oil
Chopped green onions or minced fresh rosemary, for garnish (optional)

1. Place the chicken fat in a soup pot and set over medium-high heat. When hot, add the mushrooms and sauté until they are tender and reduced in size. Add the green onions and the stock. Cover, reduce the heat, and allow to reach a simmer. Turn the heat to low.

2. Boil 4 cups of water with 2 tablespoons of salt. When the water is boiling vigorously, add the pasta. Stir, cover, and cook for 7 minutes, or until the pasta is tender but still has a bit of bite to it. Drain and drizzle the olive oil into the pasta. Stir well to coat the pasta with the oil.

3. Spoon ⅓ cup of the pasta into each soup bowl and ladle the soup over it. Serve immediately. If you wish, you may garnish with a few chopped green onions or minced rosemary.

With the success of the Chicken Broth with Cremini and Pasta (page 130), I began experimenting with a few other simple but highly effective autumn soups—using, of course, my homemade chicken stock as a base. This soup is also very light and flavorful. (If you want a richer, fuller flavored, and perhaps more robust version of this soup, I suggest you try my recipe for Fuji Apple and Gorgonzola Soup; page 128.) This soup is a perfect autumn dish, combining as it does two of the best flavors the fall has to offer—apples and onions. If you wish to omit the gorgonzola or substitute a nice creamy chèvre, go ahead and try it out!

¼ cup chicken fat or unsalted butter
2 red onions, thinly sliced lengthwise
12-ounce bottle hard apple cider
2 sweet and crisp apples, such as Honey Crisp, Fuji, Sweet Orin, Pippin, or Braeburn, peeled, cored, and sliced thin
8 cups clarified chicken stock (page 37)
Crumbled gorgonzola
Sprigs of fresh rosemary, for garnish (optional)

1. Place the chicken fat In a soup pot and set over medium-high heat. When hot, add the onions and sauté until they begin to caramelize.

2. Add the cider. Quickly stir the onions into the cider so that they become glazed with the liquid. Allow most of the cider to evaporate. Add the sliced apples and the stock and turn the

heat to low. Allow the soup to simmer until the apples become tender. Check by eating a slice of apple every few minutes. When they are no longer crisp but not falling apart, they are finished.

3. Remove the pot from the heat and ladle the soup into bowls. Top with crumbled gorgonzola and serve. If you want to garnish with an herb to spruce up the color, add a sprig of rosemary.

I had been wanting to make a cashew soup for a while when it hit me that I had seen recipes using cashews in some of the Indian cookbooks that I own. Instead of searching the recipes out, I decided to modify my Curried Cauliflower and Potato Soup (page 178). While this soup is a modification of that one, the flavor is completely different. There are a lot of cashews in this recipe because I wanted the cashews to stand out and be the main flavor throughout the soup. Their creamy and nutty flavor is a perfect balance for the curry powder and the coconut milk. This soup turned out to be rather mild, even with the curry and the peppers. It also sold very well in the autumn, when there is a mild chill in the air.

¼ teaspoon saffron threads (optional)
1 cup boiling water
½ head cauliflower, cut into bite-size pieces
6 tablespoons oil (peanut, coconut, or canola) or ghee
1 tablespoon brown mustard seeds
5 jalapeño or 8 Thai peppers, roughly chopped
1 cup whole raw cashews
2 tablespoons minced garlic

1 yellow onion, minced
1-inch piece ginger, minced
1 tablespoon kosher salt
2 tablespoons curry powder
1 pound new red potatoes, washed and cut into bite-size pieces
Two 14-ounce cans coconut milk
¼ cup lemon juice
2 tablespoons coarsely chopped cilantro

AUTUMN

1. Place the saffron threads, if using, and the boiling water in a cup. Set aside.

2. Preheat the oven to 450°F.

3. Combine the cauliflower and 3 tablespoons of the oil in a roasting pan. Toss the cauliflower to coat well with the oil. Roast until the cauliflower begins to crisp and turn golden. Check every 10 minutes and stir the cauliflower occasionally to keep it from burning. When the cauliflower is tender (a fork easily pierces through the flesh), remove the roasting pan and set it aside.

4. Meanwhile, pour the rest of the oil into a soup pot and set over high heat. When hot and beginning to smoke, add the brown mustard seeds and quickly set the lid ajar on top of the pot. When an aroma similar to popcorn emanates from the pot, add the peppers and quickly stir. When the peppers begin to look blistered and change colors, add the cashews. Stir well to coat the nuts with the oil. Allow the cashews to sauté until they begin to change color. Add the garlic and stir. When the garlic begins to change to a light golden color, add the onion. Stir well, cover, and allow to sauté for 5 minutes, or until the onion is translucent and very soft. Add the ginger, salt, and curry powder. Stir, cover, and allow to sauté for another 5 minutes, or until there is a thick liquid forming at the bottom of the soup pot.

5. Add the saffron-infused water (threads and all), the potatoes, and the coconut milk. Reduce the heat to medium and allow the potatoes to simmer until they are tender. Add the roasted cauliflower. Stir well and allow everything to simmer for another 5 minutes on medium-low heat.

6. Remove from the heat and add the lemon juice and the cilantro. Stir well and adjust to taste with salt. If this soup seems too thick you may add water to it. However, if you add water be sure to add a little salt. Serve immediately.

Sometimes I am just not in the mood for a heavy, starchy soup, and when this happens, I usually avoid potato soups. This soup came from an experiment one of those times. I had mushrooms to use and was planning on making a Potato-Leek Soup (page 118), so I decided to omit the potatoes and substitute the mushrooms instead. The big bonus about this soup versus the traditional potato-leek is the time, not to mention that the flavor is much more heady. This soup is perfect for a rainy autumn night—something we see a lot of here in Seattle!

4 tablespoons unsalted butter

2 pounds mushrooms in season, such as cremini, shiitake, white button, lobster, chanterelle, or porcini, stemmed and sliced about ⅛ inch thick

2 leeks, washed and the white-to-light green parts thinly sliced

1 tablespoon minced fresh rosemary

1 tablespoon cracked black peppercorns

4 tablespoons flour

2 cups hot water

4 cups milk

½ cup cream sherry or a sweet white wine, such as a Riesling

1 teaspoon kosher salt

1 cup heavy cream or milk, or 4 cups water

1. Melt 2 tablespoons of the butter in a soup pot over high heat. Add the sliced mushrooms. Stir to coat the mushrooms with the butter, cover the pot, and allow them to reduce by about half. When the mushrooms are tender, remove them from the pot and set aside in a small bowl.

AUTUMN

2. Without cleaning the soup pot, add the remaining 2 tablespoons of butter and allow it to melt. Add the leeks, rosemary, and peppercorns to the pot, stir well, cover, and sauté until the leeks are very wilted and tender. Remove the pot from the heat and allow the leeks to stand for about 5 minutes.

3. Add the mushrooms and stir to mix well. Add the flour and stir well to coat everything. Pour 1 cup of the hot water into the soup pot. Stir until the floury paste has thinned evenly throughout. When you reach an even consistency, add the remaining cup of hot water and the milk and repeat the stirring. Set the pot back over medium-low heat and allow the soup to reach a simmer. Stir occasionally to keep the flour from burning at the bottom of the pot.

4. Just when the soup begins to boil, reduce the heat to low, and add the sherry, salt, and cream to the pot. Stir well to evenly incorporate the cream. Cover and allow the soup to reach a simmer. Remove from the heat and serve immediately.

Luckily for us in Seattle, mushrooms are plentiful. And if you get the right mushrooms at the right time of year they can also be relatively inexpensive. When I first started making soups, I worked with dried mushrooms for extra flavor. After I realized that fresh was much, much better and much, much cheaper, I dropped the dried option. Don't get me wrong, dehydrated mushrooms work great in a pinch, but they do tend to be quite pricey.

This soup celebrates the wild and wonderful world and flavor of the mushroom. Also, this soup can be made year round as long as you use the mushrooms that are in season. This version was made during the autumn months. I used a combination of shiitake, chanterelle, portobello, cremini, hedgehog, oyster, and cauliflower mushrooms.

2 pounds assorted mushrooms
4 tablespoons unsalted butter
¼ cup dry white wine
2 cloves garlic, minced
1 teaspoon shaved black truffle (optional)
1 yellow onion, thinly sliced
1 bulb fennel, thinly sliced (optional)
4 cups Basic Vegetable Stock (page 31)
2 bay leaves
1 teaspoon kosher salt
1 teaspoon coarsely ground black peppercorns

1. Clean off any dirt or debris clinging to the mushrooms with a damp rag. Remove the gills and stem of the portobellos, if using. Slice the mushrooms about ½ inch thick.

2. Melt 2 tablespoons of the butter in a soup pot over high heat. Add the mushrooms. Stir well to coat with butter, cover, and let simmer until reduced and a broth has formed at the bottom of the pot. Add the wine, stir well, and cover for about 5 minutes. Remove from the heat, pour the mushrooms into a bowl, and set aside.

3. Return the uncleaned pot to the stove and melt the remaining 2 tablespoons of butter in it. Add the garlic and sauté until it turns golden. Add the truffle, if using, to the soup pot and sauté until a rich, earthy aroma takes over the entire kitchen, about 2 minutes.

4. Add the onion and fennel, if using. Stir well to coat. Cover and let sauté until very tender. Pour the mushrooms and their juices back into the soup pot. Stir well, then add the stock, bay leaves, salt, and peppercorns. Cover and let simmer for 20 minutes, or until just beginning to boil.

5. Remove from the heat and ladle into soup bowls. Serve immediately.

I wanted to make a hearty autumn cauliflower soup again, but I didn't want to make the same old cream of cauliflower, even though I know it is popular among the patrons of the pub. I wanted to push the cauliflower envelope. While talking to my mother one day, she mentioned that her mom used to use a ham bone when making soup. Now, I personally didn't find the suggestion of using a ham bone to be the most exciting idea, but it did remind me that I had a few pounds of pancetta (Italian cured bacon) sitting in the freezer at work. The next day I pulled it out and let it thaw. This soup is what came from combining the subtle flavors of the cauliflower, the tangy sweetness of orange, the woody flavor of rosemary, and the sweet and rich flavor of the pancetta.

6 tablespoons olive oil, plus more for roasting cauliflower
1 head cauliflower
1 pound pancetta, cut into ½-inch cubes
1 yellow onion, sliced
¼ pound shallots, minced
1 leek, washed and sliced
1 tablespoon kosher salt

1 tablespoon black peppercorns
2 tablespoons minced fresh rosemary
1 tablespoon minced fresh thyme
4 cups Basic Vegetable Stock (page 31)
½ cup cream sherry
2 cups cream
Grated zest and juice of 1 orange

1. Preheat the oven to 450°F. Coat a small roasting pan with 2 tablespoons of olive oil.

AUTUMN

2. Remove and dice the stem and leaves of the cauliflower and reserve. Cut the head in half. Separate the florets of half of the head into bite-size pieces. Chop the other half of the head into small pieces and place in a bowl along with the diced stem and leaves. Set the latter pile aside.

3. Place the cauliflower florets and the pancetta in the roasting dish. Toss gently to coat with oil. Roast until the cauliflower begins to crisp and brown on the edges, tossing occasionally to make sure nothing is charring or burning at the bottom of the roasting pan.

4. Meanwhile, pour the rest of the olive oil into a soup pot and place the pot over high heat. When the oil is hot, add the onion, shallots, and leek and stir well to evenly coat with the oil. Cover and allow the mixture to sauté until the onions become translucent and the leeks grow tender and reduce in size.

5. Add the reserved pile of cauliflower, along with the salt, pepper, rosemary, and thyme. Stir, cover, reduce the heat to medium-high, and allow to sauté until the cauliflower gets tender.

6. Add the stock, stir well, cover, and allow the soup to reach a boil. Cook for 15 minutes, or until the cauliflower is extremely soft.

7. Remove the pot from the heat. Purée the soup in batches. Press through a strainer into a storage container and discard anything that remains in the strainer. Clean out the pot and pour the puréed soup back into it.

8. Add the sherry, cream, roasted cauliflower, and pancetta, and stir well. Keep the heat at medium. Cover and allow the soup to reach a simmer. Once simmering, remove the soup pot from the heat and stir in the orange zest and juice. Allow the soup to sit for a few minutes before serving.

This autumn soup is another clarified chicken stock soup—yet another example of how versatile chicken stock can be. The big bonus about this soup is that it is relatively easy and inexpensive to make once you have the chicken stock.

I have only recently started working with hard liquor. I think the rum adds depth to this soup. Just make sure you don't use spiced rum!

> **6 tablespoons chicken fat or unsalted butter**
> **1 pound shallots, finely sliced**
> **¼ cup rum**
> **1 bulb fennel, finely sliced**
> **1 tablespoon minced fresh rosemary**
> **1 tablespoon minced fresh thyme**
> **1 tablespoon minced fresh oregano**
> **Two 14-ounce cans white beans**
> **8 cups clarified chicken stock (page 37)**

1. Melt 2 tablespoons of the chicken fat or butter over high heat in a soup pot. When hot, add the shallots. Stir well to coat with the fat. Cover the pot and allow the shallots to sauté until they begin to caramelize. Add the rum and stir well to glaze the shallots. Allow some of the liquid to evaporate, then empty the pot into a small bowl and set aside.

2. Melt the rest of the fat or butter in the pot. Add the fennel and herbs and stir to coat well.

Cover and sauté the until tender, about 10 minutes. Add the beans to the pot, along with the chicken stock. Stir well to incorporate everything. Turn the heat down to medium and allow the soup to reach a simmer.

3. Add the caramelized shallots to the simmering soup. Stir well to evenly distribute the shallots. If you want to make this soup ahead of time, omit the beans until you are reheating the soup just before serving. White beans are delicate in texture so they can fall apart and/or change color when being heated, cooled, and reheated.

Ah . . . when truffles come into season, I grow all warm and squishy on the inside. This is a somewhat pricey soup, and you need to know where to locate fresh black truffles at a "reasonably" inexpensive price. This is another broth soup that demonstrates the wonderful flavors of the late autumn months.

> 1 pound chestnuts
> ¼ cup olive oil or chicken fat
> 1 teaspoon shaved black truffle
> 1 yellow onion, thinly sliced
> 1 bulb fennel, thinly sliced
> ½ pound pancetta, thinly sliced
> 1 tablespoon minced fresh rosemary
> 1 tablespoon minced fresh thyme
> 1 teaspoon kosher salt
> 8 cups clarified chicken stock (page 37)

1. Preheat the oven to 450°F.

2. Carve small **X**s on the flat bottom of each chestnut and spread them out onto a cookie sheet. Place in the oven and roast until the skins begin to pull back from the meat inside— about 15 minutes. Remove from the oven and set aside. When the chestnuts are just cool

AUTUMN

enough to handle, use a paring knife and peel away the skins as quickly and as carefully as possible. Discard the parings and allow the nuts to cool. Slice into thin medallions and set in a container until you are ready to serve the soup.

3. Heat the oil or fat in a soup pot over high heat. When hot, add the shaved truffle. Stir and sauté until they begin to release their heady and earthy aroma. Quickly add the onion and fennel. Stir well, cover, and allow to sauté until the onion is translucent and the fennel tender.

4. Add the pancetta, rosemary, thyme, and salt to the pot. Stir again, cover, and simmer the pancetta in the juices of the onion and fennel. If the pot is dry, add a little of the stock.

5. Add the stock. Stir the soup well, cover, and lower the heat to medium. Allow the soup to reach a simmer. Serve immediately with the sliced chestnuts.

NOTE: This soup is something you want to make just before serving. It really doesn't present itself very well if it is reheated. If you don't particularly care for chestnuts, I suggest using a nice chèvre (goat cheese).

WINTER

BEET and APPLE SOUP with SOUR CREAM and FRESH DILL

1½ HOURS PREP TIME • YIELDS EIGHT 1-CUP SERVINGS

This hearty soup is served with sour cream and fresh dill. Should you find the finished soup has become a little grainy looking, add another cup of vegetable stock or water and a teaspoon of salt.

4 tablespoons unsalted butter
1 red onion, finely sliced
1 shallot, finely sliced
3 tablespoons balsamic vinegar
2 pounds beets, trimmed, peeled, and grated
2 stems fresh tarragon, 6 inches each, coarsely chopped
1 teaspoon black peppercorns
1 teaspoon kosher salt
4 cups Basic Vegetable Stock (page 31)
2 apples, peeled, cored, and finely sliced
½ cup apple cider, hard or sweet
Sour cream, for garnish
Fresh dill, finely chopped, for garnish

1. Place 2 tablespoons of the butter in a stockpot and set over medium-high heat until melted. Add the onion and shallot and sauté until golden brown and caramelized, that is, when they smell very sweet and the juices from the onion have evaporated.

2. Add the balsamic vinegar and mix well. Scrape off any onion pieces that may have stuck to the bottom of the pot.

3. Add the beets, tarragon, peppercorns, and salt. Mix well. Add the stock. Cover and let simmer until everything begins to fall apart, about 45 minutes to 1 hour.

4. Once the beets are extremely soft, purée the soup in batches. Strain the purée and discard anything that does not pass through the strainer. Set aside.

5. Clean the stockpot. Add the remaining 2 tablespoons of butter and let melt over medium-high heat. Add the apples and stir well. Cover and let simmer for 10 minutes.

6. Add the apple cider, mix well, and cover. Cook until the apples are very tender but not falling apart.

7. Add the puréed beets to the apples. Mix well.

8. Serve topped with sour cream and fresh dill.

GREEN CHILE STEW

1 HOUR PREP TIME • YIELDS TEN 1-CUP SERVINGS

This stew will heat up your belly and clear your head. And it is full of vitamins, too! There is a bit of nostalgia associated with green chilies for me, memories of New Mexican street corners with the gas-fired roasting barrels, the smell of green chilies wafting through my friends' houses, warm homemade tortillas, and the traditional posole. How can I forget?

You can replace all or part of the pinto beans with beef, pork, or chicken in this recipe; just make sure the meat is thoroughly cooked before adding.

¼ cup olive oil
2 tablespoons minced garlic
1 yellow onion, sliced
3 ribs celery, sliced
Kosher salt
2 tablespoons chopped fresh oregano
2 bay leaves
1 teaspoon coriander seeds,
 toasted and ground
1½ teaspoons cumin seeds,
 toasted and ground

12 to 15 medium Roma tomatoes,
 peeled, seeded, and coarsely
 chopped, or a 32-ounce can diced
 tomatoes
½ pound green chilies, preferably from
 Hatch, New Mexico, roasted, peeled,
 seeded, and chopped
1 pound potatoes, cubed
4 cups Basic Vegetable Stock
 (page 31)
16-ounce can pinto beans,
 drained and rinsed
Flour tortillas

1. Melt the olive oil in a soup pot over medium heat. Add the garlic and sauté until golden. Add the onion, celery, and 1 teaspoon salt. Stir to coat with oil and cover. Let simmer for 15 minutes, or until the celery releases its liquid. Add the oregano and spices. Stir well, cover, and let the mixture cook for another 5 minutes.

2. Add the tomatoes and green chilies and stir well. Cover and let simmer for 10 to 15 minutes.

3. Add the potatoes, another teaspoon salt, and the stock. Stir well to mix everything together. Cover and let the stock reach a boil. Stir occasionally to keep the bottom from burning. Let cook until the potatoes are tender and can be pierced easily with a fork. If the mixture is too thick, add stock until the level of the liquid is equal to the level of the potatoes.

4. Add the pinto beans and stir well. Cover and cook for another 10 minutes, or until the beans are warmed through.

5. Remove from heat and serve immediately with warm, buttered flour tortillas.

WINTER

CORN AND GREEN CHILE CHOWDER

1½ HOURS PREP TIME • YIELDS TEN 1-CUP SERVINGS

This was my first soup ever. I've made it so many times—with so many variations and experimentations—I've lost count. It is still a wonderful winter soup with the cream, the potatoes, and the hot green chilies. My mouth waters just thinking about it.

¼ cup unsalted butter
2 tablespoons minced garlic
1 yellow onion, diced
2 ribs celery, sliced
2 tablespoons chopped fresh oregano
1 teaspoon cumin seeds, toasted and ground
1 teaspoon coriander seeds, toasted and ground
1 teaspoon black peppercorns, cracked
¼ cup flour
2 cups Basic Vegetable Stock (page 31) or Basic Chicken Stock (page 33)

16-ounce can sweet corn, drained
½ pound green chilies, preferably from Hatch, New Mexico, roasted, peeled, deveined, seeded, and chopped
6-ounce can roasted red peppers, drained and cut into thin strips
1½ pounds potatoes, red or Yukon gold, washed and cut into ½-inch cubes
Kosher salt
½ cup cream
2 cups milk
Baguette or flour tortillas, for serving
Sliced green chile and roasted red pepper, for garnish (optional)

1. Melt the butter in a soup pot. Add the garlic and sauté until golden. Add the onion and celery. Stir to coat with butter. Cover and let cook over medium-high heat until the liquids are released. Add the herbs, spices, and peppercorns and stir well. Cover and let simmer for 5 minutes. Add the flour and mix until the contents of the pot are coated and all lumps of flour are gone. Add the stock in 1-cup portions. Stir the soup well after each addition.

2. Add the corn, green chilies, and red peppers. Stir well, cover, and simmer until the soup begins to boil. Add the potatoes and 2 teaspoons salt. Stir well, cover, and reduce the heat to medium. Cook for 15 to 20 minutes, or until the potatoes are tender and can be easily pierced with a fork. Stir occasionally to make sure nothing burns and sticks to the bottom of the pot.

3. Remove from the heat. Add the cream and the milk and stir well. Adjust to taste with salt and pepper. If the soup is too thick, add more stock.

4. Serve hot with a crusty baguette or warmed tortillas. If you want to add a garnish, top with thin strips of sliced green chile and roasted red pepper.

CREAM of GREEN CHILE SOUP
2 HOURS PREP TIME • YIELDS TEN 1-CUP SERVINGS

The best green chilies come from Hatch Valley, New Mexico, harvested in September. By the end of autumn every home in New Mexico has at least a hundred pounds of green chilies sitting in the freezer for the coming year. Well, maybe not every home, but probably most. Warn your guests. These little numbers can be *muy picante!*

1 large baking potato
¼ cup unsalted butter
1 tablespoon minced garlic
1 yellow onion, finely sliced
2 ribs celery, finely sliced
Kosher salt
1 teaspoon black peppercorns, cracked
1 teaspoon coriander seeds, toasted and ground
2 teaspoons cumin seeds, toasted and ground

2 tablespoons chopped fresh oregano
½ pound green chilies, preferably from Hatch, New Mexico, roasted, peeled, deveined, seeded, and chopped
6 cups Basic Vegetable Stock (page 31)
4 cups cream
Flour tortillas
Chopped oregano and roasted red peppers, for garnish

1. Preheat the oven to 550°F.

2. Roast the potato for about 40 minutes, or until a fork or knife is easily inserted. Set aside to cool.

3. Melt the butter in a soup pot over medium-high heat. Add the garlic and sauté until golden brown. Add the onion, celery, and 1 teaspoon salt. Mix well, cover, and cook until the vegetables reduce in volume and the onion is very soft and translucent.

4. Add the black pepper, coriander, cumin, and oregano. Mix well. Add the green chilies and 2 cups of the stock. Stir well and cover. Let simmer for roughly 30 minutes, stirring occasionally so nothing sticks and burns.

5. Meanwhile, cut the potato in half lengthwise. With a large spoon, scoop the flesh out of the potato and place it in a food processor. Purée the potato by slowly adding 2 cups of the stock until it has a smooth and creamy consistency. Remove from the food processor and set aside.

6. Once all the vegetables have softened considerably, remove the pot from the heat. In batches, purée this mixture. Then press each batch through a strainer over a storage container. Discard anything that remains in the strainer.

7. Clean out the pot. Return to it the puréed soup, the puréed potatoes, and the cream. If the soup seems too thick, add some of the remaining stock to thin it out. Remove from the heat. Adjust to taste with salt and pepper. Chill in the refrigerator overnight to meld flavors.

8. To serve, reheat to a simmer. Serve with warm tortillas and garnish with chopped oregano and sliced roasted red peppers.

NIGERIAN YAM SOUP
1 HOUR PREP TIME • YIELDS TEN 1-CUP SERVINGS

Fresh and plentiful in winter, habañero peppers give a great flavor as well as intense heat to this light soup. They are very hot! Nothing is wrong with a little sweat, but some people do have sensitive mouths. You may wish to offer yogurt along with the soup to help cut the heat of the habañeros. I personally prefer to use the red garnet variety of yam, but, if you cannot locate these or even true yams, you can easily substitute sweet potatoes.

> ¼ cup unsalted butter
> 2 bunches green onions, chopped
> Kosher salt
> 1 or 2 habañero peppers, seeded and chopped
> 2 pounds yams, peeled, grated, and soaking in cold water
> 6 cups Basic Vegetable Stock (page 31)
> Green onions and yogurt, for garnish

1. Melt the butter in a soup pot over medium-high heat. Add the green onions and mix well. Add 1 teaspoon salt and mix well. Cover and let the green onions reduce for about 5 to 10 minutes. Add the peppers. Sauté for 5 more minutes. Add the grated yams and about 2 teaspoons salt, replace the lid, lower the heat to medium, and let the volume of the yams reduce.

2. Add 2 cups of the stock. Cover and let simmer for 30 minutes, or until the yams are mushy and break apart when pressed between two fingers.

S.O.U.P.S.

3. Purée in batches, pressing each batch through a strainer into a storage container. Discard anything that remains in the strainer. Clean out the pot.

4. Add the rest of the stock to the yams. Return to the pot. Let the soup simmer over medium to low heat until it just begins to boil.

5. Remove from the heat and adjust salt to taste. Let chill overnight to meld the flavors.

6. To serve, reheat to a simmer and garnish with thinly sliced green onions and a dollop of yogurt.

MASALA DAAL
2 HOURS PREP TIME • YIELDS TWELVE 1-CUP SERVINGS

This soup is made in two parts: the lentils and the vegetables. If you don't want the spicy heat, omit the peppers. If you don't have peppers, use cayenne. But while you add the peppers to the vegetable mixture, you add cayenne to the boiling water the lentils cook in.

2 sticks cinnamon
10 cloves
10 cardamom pods
10 black peppercorns
1 teaspoon fenugreek
1 teaspoon cumin seeds
2 teaspoons coriander seeds
2 tablespoons canola oil or ghee
1 tablespoon brown mustard seeds
Pinch of asafetida
2 tablespoons minced garlic

1 yellow onion, finely chopped
1-inch piece ginger,
    peeled and minced
2 to 3 jalapeño, serrano, or
    Thai peppers, seeded and minced
32-ounce can diced tomato
1 teaspoon turmeric
Cayenne (optional)
2 cups lentils, soaked at least 2 hours
½ cup lemon juice
1 bunch cilantro, leaves only,
    coarsely chopped

1. Individually toast the first seven spices in a small, hot skillet. Let cool and grind to a powder. Blend together and set aside.

2. Heat the canola oil or melt the ghee in a 1½-quart heavy-bottomed saucepan over high heat until very hot.

3. With the lid of the pan in one hand, pour the brown mustard seeds into the oil and immediately cover. When the popping subsides, remove the lid. Add the asafetida and shake the pan. Add the garlic and give the pot another shake. Add the onion and immediately stir to mix. Lower the heat, cover, and let cook for 5 minutes, or until the onion is golden brown.

4. Add the ginger and peppers. Mix well, cover, lower the heat to medium, and cook for about 5 more minutes.

5. Add the diced tomatoes and the spices (except the turmeric and cayenne, if using). Mix well and cover. Let simmer until the mixture begins to bubble. Remove from the heat and set aside.

6. Fill a soup pot with 4 quarts of fresh water, the turmeric, and cayenne. Cover and let it reach a boil over high heat.

7. Drain and rinse the soaked lentils, then add to the boiling water. Stir to keep the lentils from sticking to the bottom. Partially cover the pot and let the lentils cook for 20 minutes, or until the lentils are soft but not mushy.

8. Place a storage container in the sink with a colander sitting on top of it. Once the lentils are ready, carefully pour the lentils and water into the colander. Once all the water has passed through the colander and into the storage container, put the lentils back in the pot along with the tomato mixture and mix well.

9. Slowly add the cooking liquid from the lentils to the soup pot with the tomatoes and lentils until the desired consistency is reached. Discard extra liquid. Mix well and let simmer for about 10 minutes.

10. Remove from the heat and stir in the lemon juice and cilantro. Serve at once.

PEANUT AND YAM SOUP

1 HOUR PREP TIME • YIELDS TWELVE 1-CUP SERVINGS

This soup should be nice and thick and a pretty, orange color. Hearty and filling, it makes a great dipping soup and becomes a meal in itself when served with lots of bread. It will have a little heat due to the cayenne, but it should not be too overwhelming.

¼ cup unsalted butter
1 yellow onion, finely sliced
2 ribs celery, finely sliced
1 teaspoon cayenne
Kosher salt
2 pounds yams, preferably Red Garnets, peeled, grated, and soaking in water,
 or roasted, peeled, and puréed
4 cups Basic Vegetable Stock (page 31)
1 cup natural peanut butter, freshly ground (no sugar)
Chopped honey-roasted peanuts, for garnish
Bread, for serving

1. Melt the butter in a soup pot over medium-high heat. Add the onion, celery, cayenne, and 1 tablespoon salt. Mix well and cover. Let simmer for about 10 minutes, stirring occasionally. If the onion begins to burn, reduce the heat to medium.

2. Drain the yams and add them in three separate batches with 1 teaspoon salt per batch. Stir well, cover, and let volume reduce, about 10 minutes, with each addition. If using roasted yams, pour the puréed yams into the pot, stir well, and continue with Step 4.

3. Once all of the yams are in the pot, add stock until you can see it right below the surface of the yams. Stir well and cover. Let cook until the yams are mushy and fall apart when pressed between two of your fingers.

4. In batches in a food processor, purée the yams with a heaping scoop of peanut butter. Press through a strainer into a storage container. Discard anything that remains in the strainer.

5. Wash out the pot and replace the soup. Put it back on the heat and add any remaining stock to help thin out the soup, if needed. Mix well and cover. Let it reach a simmer.

6. Top the soup with chopped honey-roasted peanuts and serve with plenty of bread.

WINTER

CREAM of BROCCOLI SOUP with ORANGE and CUMIN

1 HOUR PREP TIME • YIELDS TWELVE 1-CUP SERVINGS

Both broccoli and oranges are abundant in the winter. The subtle flavor of the broccoli along with the zippy tang of oranges and the earthy quality of cumin makes a very pleasant and relaxing soup for a cold winter's night. If you want to be a bit decadent, garnish with a handful of grated cheddar cheese.

> 2 teaspoons cumin seeds, whole
> ¼ pound slivered almonds
> ¼ cup unsalted butter
> 2 tablespoons minced garlic
> 1 large yellow onion, finely sliced
> Kosher salt
> 1½ to 2 pounds broccoli, stemmed, half of the florets reserved, and half finely chopped
> 4 cups Basic Vegetable Stock (page 31)
> 4 cups cream
> Grated zest of 1 orange
> 1 teaspoon white peppercorns, cracked
> Grated cheddar cheese and ¼ cup toasted slivered almonds, for garnish

1. Toast the cumin seeds until they are a couple of shades darker. Let cool and grind into a powder. Set aside. Toast the almonds until golden. Let cool and grind until fine. Set aside.

2. Melt the butter in a soup pot. Add the garlic and onion and 1 teaspoon salt. Mix well, cover, and let simmer until onions become soft and translucent.

3. Add the ground almonds and mix. Add the chopped broccoli and stir well. Add 1 teaspoon salt and half of the stock and cover. Lower heat to medium and simmer for about 30 minutes, or until all the vegetables begin to get mushy.

4. In batches, purée the broccoli and onion mixture. Pour each batch through a strainer into a storage container. Discard anything that remains in the strainer. Clean the pot.

5. Return the soup to the pot. Add the reserved broccoli florets, the cream, and as much stock as you can fit into the pot without it overflowing. Mix well.

6. Add the toasted cumin seeds and the orange zest to the soup. Stir well. Cover and cook until the soup thickens slightly.

7. Remove from the heat and adjust the flavor with salt and white pepper.

8. Serve with grated cheddar cheese and/or chopped almonds.

WINTER

This soup is very hearty and nutty in flavor. Coconut, pepper, and coriander are a great flavor combination. As far as the barrel-shaped mooth lentil goes, it can be found in Indian grocery stores and must be picked clean for any tiny stones, sticks, and dirt, but is well worth the effort.

¼ cup ghee or coconut, peanut, or canola oil
1 teaspoon brown mustard seeds
Pinch asafetida
2 tablespoons minced garlic
1 yellow onion, finely chopped
2 teaspoons coriander seeds, toasted and ground
1 cup shredded unsweetened coconut
3 to 5 jalapeño, serrano, or Thai peppers, seeded and minced
½ teaspoon turmeric
1 pound mooth lentils, soaked for 12 hours and sprouted for 8 to 12 hours
14-ounce can coconut milk
Lemon juice
Black onion seeds or chopped fresh cilantro and shredded and
     toasted coconut, for garnish

1. Heat the ghee or oil in a soup pot. When very hot, hold the lid in one hand and pour the mustard seeds into the ghee, give the pot a shake, and immediately cover with the lid. When the popping subsides, remove the lid. Add the asafetida and the minced garlic and stir well. Once the garlic has turned golden, add the onion and stir well. Cover and let sizzle for 10 minutes.

2. Add the coriander, coconut, peppers, and turmeric. Stir well, cover, and let simmer for 5 more minutes.

3. Drain and rinse the sprouted lentils. Add and stir well. Add the coconut milk and enough water to reach about 1 inch above the lentils. Cover and let simmer for about 1 hour, or until the lentils are tender but not mushy. Taste and adjust the flavor with lemon juice.

4. Serve with a sprinkling of black onion seeds or a little chopped cilantro and toasted shredded coconut.

MOROCCAN LENTIL SOUP
2 HOURS PREP TIME • YIELDS TWELVE 1-CUP SERVINGS

A lovely warming soup for winter, chock full of lentils, spices, and vegetables. So hearty one will struggle to pull up a spoon with only broth in it. I like the multicolored effect of the green, red, yellow, and orange bell peppers, white onions, and red tomatoes. This is a delightful soup!

¼ cup olive oil
2 tablespoons minced garlic
½ yellow onion, thinly sliced
1 small rib celery, sliced
1 small carrot, sliced
1 teaspoon cumin seeds,
  toasted and ground
1 teaspoon coriander seeds,
  toasted and ground
Kosher salt
32-ounce can diced tomatoes,
  with juice
½ green bell pepper,
  cut into ½-inch pieces

½ red bell pepper,
  cut into ½-inch pieces
½ yellow bell pepper,
  cut into ½-inch pieces
½ orange bell pepper,
  cut into ½-inch pieces
1-inch piece ginger,
  peeled and minced
½ teaspoon cayenne
1 tablespoon turmeric
2 cups Petit French lentils,
  soaked at least 2 hours
1 tablespoon lemon juice
Cilantro leaves, for garnish

1. Heat the olive oil in a soup pot over high heat. Add the garlic and stir well. When it begins to turn golden, add the onion and stir well. Cover and let sizzle for 5 minutes.

2. Add the celery, carrot, cumin, coriander, and 2 teaspoons salt. Stir well. Lower the heat to medium, cover, and let cook for about 10 minutes.

3. Add the tomatoes and their juice, the bell peppers, and ½ cup of water, to the onion mixture. Stir well. Cover and simmer for another 20 minutes, or until the mixture bubbles and steams. Remove from the heat.

4. Fill another pot with 4 cups of water, cover, and bring to a boil. Add the ginger, cayenne, and turmeric.

5. Drain and rinse the lentils. Place the cleaned lentils in the boiling water. Cover and cook for 15 to 30 minutes, or until they are just tender.

6. Place a colander over a container large enough to hold the water from cooking the lentils. Strain the lentils through the colander, reserving the water.

7. Place the tomato mixture back on the heat. Add the lentils and stir well. Add just enough of the reserved water to reach the top of the lentils. Stir well and heat to a simmer. Remove from the heat and add the lemon juice. Stir well to incorporate.

8. Serve garnished with cilantro.

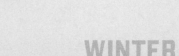

BRAZILIAN BLACK BEAN SOUP
12 HOURS PREP TIME • YIELDS TWELVE 1-CUP SERVINGS

They served this soup regularly at one of my first jobs, and I loved its subtle undertones. I tried many times to make it and failed miserably. This special soup remained a mystery to me for the longest time until I realized the amount of cloves needs to be very minimal, and the orange must be added at the very end.

¼ cup canola oil
2 tablespoons minced garlic
1 red onion, chopped
1 to 3 jalapeño or serrano peppers, seeded and minced
2 teaspoons coriander seeds, toasted and coarsely ground
1 teaspoon ground cinnamon
Pinch of ground cloves
32-ounce can diced tomatoes, with juice
6 cups Basic Vegetable Stock (page 31)
2 cups dried black beans, soaked overnight
Grated zest and juice of 1 orange
¼ bunch cilantro, washed, stemmed, and coarsely chopped, plus more for garnish
Sour cream and sliced roasted red pepper, for garnish

1. Heat the oil in a soup pot over high heat. Add the garlic and sauté until golden. Add the onion and stir well. Cover and cook for 5 minutes, or until the onion becomes translucent.

2. Add the peppers and the spices. Stir well, cover, and cook for another 5 minutes. Add the tomatoes, their juice, and the stock. Stir well and cover. Simmer for another 10 minutes.

3. Rinse the black beans under cold water until the water pouring through is clear. Add the beans and stir well. Cover the soup and let it reach a boil. Stir the soup occasionally to make sure nothing sticks to the bottom. Reduce the heat to medium-low and let the soup cook for about 45 minutes, or until the beans are very soft. Remove the pot from the heat.

4. Add the orange zest, orange juice, and cilantro and stir well. Do not let the soup boil after the orange is added; it can cause bitterness.

5. Serve the soup with a dollop of sour cream, sliced roasted red pepper, and chopped cilantro.

WINTER

While making these soups I came to realize that any soup that involves nuts, be they peanuts, cashews, walnuts, or almonds, tends to become quite a decadent treat. This soup is a creamy delicious meal that is perfect for the cooler months of autumn and winter. As it is quite rich, I really can't suggest offering large portions to people—especially if it is going to be served with other things. You can make this particular soup with any kind of nut, I suppose, but I find that pecans have the texture and flavor that I prefer. If you want to cut costs, you can do half pecans and half walnuts. I don't suggest using only walnuts since their flavor, to me, isn't as pronounced.

¼ cup olive, pecan, walnut, peanut, or canola oil
2 tablespoons minced garlic
1 large shallot, minced
1 yellow onion, minced
1 teaspoon cayenne, or 2 jalapeños, minced (optional)
1½ pounds pecans, shelled and toasted
½ cup dry white wine
4 cups Basic Vegetable Stock (page 31)
1 tablespoon kosher salt
1 tablespoon cracked black peppercorns
2 cups heavy cream
Sliced green onions and toasted chopped pecans, for garnish

1. Heat the oil in a soup pot over medium-high heat. Add the garlic. Stir well and sauté until the garlic begins to turn golden. Add the shallot and onion. Stir well, cover, and allow to sauté until the onions turn translucent. Add the cayenne or jalapeños, if using.

2. Add the pecans, wine, stock, salt, and pepper. Stir well and cover the pot. Allow to simmer over medium heat for about 40 minutes, or until the pecans become mushy. Stir occasionally, making sure that the nuts are not burning at the bottom of the soup pot.

3. When the pecans begin to fall apart, remove the soup pot from the heat and transfer the soup in batches to the food processor. Purée and then press through a strainer. Discard anything that remains in the strainer. When all of the soup has been puréed, clean out the soup pot and pour the soup back in. Stir in the cream and allow the soup to simmer over low heat until it thickens. Taste and adjust with salt and pepper if needed.

4. To serve, garnish the bowl with a small handful of thinly sliced green onions and toasted pecans.

This is a wonderfully spicy, rich, and flavorful soup. The first part of this recipe is going to make enough mole for many batches. You can freeze or jar what you don't use. You shouldn't have difficulty finding dried chilies; if, however, you cannot locate them, I suggest using ancho chilies, which are probably going to be easier to find than any of the other types.

MOLE SAUCE
4 ounces cascabel chilies, stemmed and seeded
4 ounces pasilla negro chilies, stemmed and seeded
4 ounces ancho chilies, stemmed and seeded
4 ounces pasilla Oaxaca chilies, stemmed and seeded
4 ounces chipotle chilies, stemmed and seeded
4 ounces aji amarillo chilies, stemmed and seeded
4 ounces chilcostle chilies, stemmed and seeded
4 ounces guajillo chilies, stemmed and seeded
1 cup unsalted butter
1 cup chopped fresh garlic
1½ cups shallots, roughly chopped
8 yellow onions, thinly sliced
3 tablespoons kosher salt
1 tablespoon black peppercorns
8 to 10 bay leaves, crumbled
2 tablespoons roasted and ground cumin seeds

1 tablespoon ground cinnamon
1 tablespoon garlic powder
1 tablespoon ground star anise
2 tablespoons red chile powder
2 tablespoons cocoa powder
1½ cups flour
8 cups Basic Vegetable Stock (page 31)
1 cup roasted garlic (page 19)
2 cups natural almond butter

CHICKEN MOLE
Three 6-ounce chicken breasts, skinless and boneless
½ cup olive, canola, corn, or vegetable oil
1½ pounds new red potatoes, washed and cut into ½-inch cubes
1 yellow onion, thinly sliced
1 tablespoon kosher salt
2 cups mole sauce
4 cups Basic Chicken Stock (page 33) or water from poaching the chicken breasts
Warm tortillas, for serving

1. For the mole sauce, trim the chilies and set them aside in a large bowl. Melt the butter in a large stockpot over medium-high heat. Add the garlic. Stir well and allow to sauté until the garlic turns golden. Add the shallots. Stir well, cover, and allow to sauté until the shallots turn translucent and become soft. Add the onions. Stir well, cover, and allow to sauté until they turn translucent and soft. Add the salt, peppercorns, bay leaves, the spices, and cocoa powder. Stir well, cover, and allow to sauté for a few minutes to release their flavor.

2. Add all the chilies, in batches if necessary. Stir in each batch so that they are covered with the onion/spice mixture. As the chilies begin to wilt and become soft, add more chilies. Repeat until all of the chilies are in the stockpot. Cover and allow the entire mixture to simmer and cook in its juices for about 20 minutes. Stir occasionally to make sure that nothing is burning.

3. Add the flour, stirring well to incorporate and remove any lumps. Add the stock, roasted garlic purée, and the almond butter. Cover and allow to simmer for about 30 minutes.

4. Remove from the heat. Allow to cool for a few minutes. Purée in batches in the food processor. Press through a strainer or a sieve. Discard anything that remains in the strainer. The resulting sauce should be quite thick and almost pasty. Adjust the salt if necessary. Store in 2-cup portions.

5. For the chicken mole, preheat the oven to 450°F.

6. Place the chicken breasts in a shallow pan filled with 2 cups of water. Cover with aluminum foil or a glass lid. Roast for about 30 minutes, or until the chicken is white and cooked through. Remove from the oven and allow to cool until it is easy to handle.

7. Remove the chicken from the water and place it in the refrigerator for quick cooling. Save the cooking water for the soup. Once the chicken is thoroughly cooled, shred it.

8. Meanwhile, heat the oil in a soup pot. Add the potatoes, a few at a time, and fry in the oil. When the potatoes' skins begin to shrivel and the flesh begins to turn brown, remove from the oil and put them on a paper towel–lined plate to absorb any excess oil. Continue until all the potatoes are fried.

9. If there is no oil left in the pot, add a couple of tablespoons. Add the onion and sauté until it wilts and turns translucent. Add the fried potatoes, chicken, and salt. Stir well. Cover and allow to simmer for a few minutes.

10. Add the mole sauce and the stock. Stir well to blend all ingredients together. Cover and allow to reach a boil. Reduce the heat to low and let simmer for 15 minutes, or until you begin to see an oily surface forming on top of the soup.

11. Serve the soup with warm tortillas.

This is a soup a coworker introduced to me. I had to change the recipe; otherwise it would be hers and not mine! If you want to make this vegan, replace the ghee with oil.

Tamarind paste can be found in most health-food stores. The curry leaves are the only hard-to-find item. Sadly, there really is nothing that can compare to their flavor or aroma. However, you can find these little gems at many Asian produce markets.

1 cup grated unsweetened coconut, preferably fresh
6 cloves garlic
1 teaspoon cumin or black cumin seeds, toasted and ground
6 large tomatoes, peeled, seeded, and coarsely chopped
8-ounce jar tamarind paste
1 tablespoon kosher salt
1 teaspoon curry powder
¼ cup ghee or canola oil
1 teaspoon black mustard seeds
4 to 8 Thai peppers, sliced thin
12 curry leaves, or ¼ cup dried fenugreek leaves or cilantro leaves
3 tablespoons light brown sugar
¼ cup lemon juice

1. Purée the coconut, garlic, and cumin in the food processor. Add enough water to make a thick but wet paste. Remove from the processor.

2. Combine the tomatoes, tamarind paste, salt, and curry powder in a soup pot and stir well. Add 3 cups of water and allow to reach a boil over medium-high heat. Reduce the heat and let the tomatoes simmer for 15 minutes. Purée the tomatoes and set aside.

3. Clean out the soup pot and dry it well. Melt the ghee over medium-high heat. Add the mustard seeds and immediately cover. When the spattering subsides and the aroma of popcorn is noticeable, give the pot a shake and then add the peppers. Stir until the skins of the peppers look blistered. Add the curry leaves or fenugreek, if using. They make a lot of noise and the oil may splash up a bit so keep your face turned away from the pot while adding them. Stir until they are well coated.

4. Add the coconut purée and stir well. Allow to sauté until the coconut paste begins to become obviously aromatic. Add the puréed tomatoes. Stir well, cover, and allow to simmer for roughly 10 minutes, or just until the soup begins to boil. Remove from the heat and add the sugar, lemon juice, and cilantro leaves, if using. Stir well and serve.

CREAM OF WILD MUSHROOM SOUP
1 HOUR PREP TIME • YIELDS FOUR TO EIGHT 1-CUP SERVINGS

If you like mushrooms and you have already tried the Cream of Mushroom Soup (page 114) *and* you feel like spending perhaps a bit more money to try more unusual kinds of mushrooms, I suggest you try this variation. This soup is delightfully easy and very rich. As you will notice, the primary ingredient is mushrooms. I want to make sure that when someone is eating this soup he or she will say, "My! There are a lot of mushrooms in this soup!" The shallots add a nice sweet caramelized flavor. To heighten the flavor add a couple of tablespoons of white wine vinegar to the mushrooms and shallots after they have reduced.

¼ cup unsalted butter

4 shallots, minced

2 pounds assorted wild mushrooms, stemmed, cleaned with a damp cloth, and thickly sliced

2 tablespoons white wine vinegar (optional)

¼ cup flour

½ cup white wine

1 tablespoon kosher salt

2 teaspoons cracked black peppercorns

1 tablespoon chopped fresh rosemary

¼ to ½ teaspoon ground cloves

1 tablespoon grated orange zest

4 cups Basic Vegetable Stock (page 31)

2 cups heavy cream

1. Melt the butter in a soup pot over medium-high heat. Add the shallots, stir, and cover. Sauté until they are well reduced and begin to caramelize.

2. Add the mushrooms. Stir, cover, and let sauté until reduced by half. Add the vinegar, if using, and stir well. Cover and allow the vinegar to mix with the juices of the mushrooms and shallots for a couple of minutes.

3. At this point there should be a broth forming at the bottom of the pot. Add the flour and stir well. Make sure that you dissolve all the clumps of flour before continuing. Once the lumps are broken up and the mushrooms and shallots are coated with the flour, add the wine. Stir well.

4. Lower the heat to medium. Add the salt, peppercorns, rosemary, cloves, orange zest, and stock. Stir well, cover, and let simmer until just beginning to boil. Add the cream and stir to blend well. Simmer for about 10 minutes. Do not let boil. Serve immediately.

WINTER

CURRIED CAULIFLOWER AND POTATO SOUP
1 HOUR PREP TIME • YIELDS FOUR TO EIGHT 1-CUP SERVINGS

Ahhh . . . cauliflower and potatoes, these are two subtle flavors that seem to lend themselves to a wide array of spices and other additions. This soup is the precursor to the Curried Cashew and Cauliflower Soup (page 133). While similar in ingredients, this soup is a bit lighter than the cashew version.

4 tablespoons ghee or vegetable oil
   (not peanut or olive oil)
4 large garlic cloves, minced
1-inch piece of ginger,
   peeled and minced
1 yellow onion, thinly sliced
1 cauliflower, separate head from stem
   and leaves, cut florets into ½- x ½-
   inch pieces, stem and leaves thinly
   sliced, kept in 2 piles
2 tablespoons curry powder
4 cups Basic Vegetable Stock
   (page 31)

Kosher salt
1 teaspoon brown mustard seeds
5 small jalapeño or Thai peppers,
   coarsely chopped, or more to taste
½ cup slivered almonds
3 Yukon Gold potatoes, washed and
   cut into ½- x ½-inch pieces,
   soaked in cold water
16-ounce can coconut milk
2 tablespoons lemon juice
Cilantro and diced tomatoes,
   for garnish

1. Heat 2 tablespoons of the ghee in a soup pot over high heat. Add the garlic, stir well, and sauté until dark gold or almost brown. Add the ginger and onion. Mix well, cover, and sauté until the onion begins to turn golden or brown and translucent.

2. Add the sliced stems and leaves of the cauliflower along with the curry powder. Stir well, cover, and allow to sauté until the stems and leaves begin to release their water. Stir again and add just enough stock to reach the top of the vegetables. Stir well to scrape up any of the vegetables stuck to the bottom of the pot. Add 1 teaspoon salt, stir once more, then cover and cook for about 30 minutes, or until the cauliflower is soft. Remove from the heat.

3. In batches, purée and strain. Place in a bowl and set aside.

4. Clean out the pot. Set back on the heat and melt the remaining 2 tablespoons of ghee. When the ghee begins to smoke, add the mustard seeds with one hand and cover with the lid in the other hand. When the mustard seeds have stopped popping, remove the lid from the pot and continue.

5. Put the peppers in the oil, give the pot a quick shake, and cover for a few minutes. When the peppers look blistered, add the almonds. Give another shake to the pot, cover, and simmer for a few more minutes. Add the potatoes. Stir well to coat with the oil, seeds, and peppers. Cover and allow the potatoes to fry for about 10 to 15 minutes, checking occasionally to make sure the almonds and peppers are not burning or sticking to the bottom of the pot. Add the cut-up cauliflower florets and stir well. Cover and let simmer for another 10 minutes, or until the cauliflower just starts to get tender. Add the puréed vegetables, the coconut milk, and enough stock to keep the soup from becoming too thick. Stir well, cover, and cook until the potatoes are tender enough to be pierced with a fork.

6. Remove from the heat, stir in the lemon juice, and serve immediately. Garnish, if you wish, with fresh cilantro and/or tomatoes.

POTATO-LEEK SOUP with CARAMELIZED FENNEL and VODKA

1 HOUR PREP TIME • YIELDS TWELVE TO SIXTEEN 1-CUP SERVINGS

Potato-leek is a lovely traditional soup that lends itself to modifications quite easily. This particular one is probably my personal favorite. It takes the richness of the original and pushes it over the edge. The caramelizing of the fennel helps subdue the natural anise flavor, which can overpower everything else. The vodka must be potato vodka, so when using, make sure that the vodka you have is not a rice or grain product.

½ cup unsalted butter
1 bulb fennel, finely sliced
¼ cup vodka
4 leeks, dark green part of the stem removed, finely sliced, and rinsed
1 tablespoon minced fresh rosemary
1 bunch green onions, sliced
½ cup flour
2 cups hot water
2 cups Basic Vegetable Stock (page 31)
1 tablespoon kosher salt
1 tablespoon cracked black peppercorns
1 pound red new potatoes, washed and finely sliced
1 cup cream
2 cups milk

1. Preheat the oven to 450°F.

2. Set a small roasting pan in the oven and melt half of the butter in it. Add the fennel to the pan and stir well to coat with the butter. Cover with aluminum foil or a lid and sauté, occasionally removing the pan from the oven and stirring the fennel to keep it from burning or charring, until the fennel is tender, glazed, and has crispy browned edges, up to 45 minutes. Add the vodka to the roasting pan and stir well to coat the fennel. Remove the aluminum foil and place the pan back in the oven for a few minutes. When most of the liquid has evaporated, remove the roasting pan from the oven and set aside.

3. Meanwhile, heat the remaining ¼ cup of the butter in a soup pot over high heat. Add the leeks, rosemary, and green onions. Stir well, cover, and allow to sauté until they reduce in volume and grow extremely tender. Remove the soup pot from the heat and quickly stir in the flour. Make sure there are no lumps of flour remaining in the pot but there is a very thick paste of flour and butter coating the leeks and green onions. Add the hot water. Stir well to thin the paste out. Add the stock, salt, and pepper and stir again to thin the paste out and to break up any lumps that may still exist.

4. Add the potatoes. Stir well, cover, return the pot to the heat, and allow the soup to reach a boil. Reduce the heat to medium and stir occasionally to keep the potatoes from sticking to the bottom of the pot. Reduce the heat to medium-low or even low if necessary.

5. Once the potatoes are tender or al dente (your choice), add the cream, milk, and the caramelized fennel. Stir well to incorporate everything. Bring it back to a simmer and serve immediately.

TAFFY'S PEPPER POT WITH PORK AND RED CABBAGE
1 TO 1½ HOURS PREP TIME • YIELDS TWELVE TO SIXTEEN 1-CUP SERVINGS

Some people might feel that the original Taffy's Pepper Pot (page 60) doesn't have enough substance to it. This version does. I suggest adding the shredded pork to the soup right before serving. That way the pork will retain its texture instead of turning stringy and tough. Bear in mind that this soup is extremely hot!

¼ cup peanut oil
Four 4-ounce cuts pork shoulder,
  any fat removed
Flour, for dredging
¼ cup sesame oil
8 cloves garlic, sliced thin
1 yellow onion, sliced
1 jalapeño pepper, stemmed,
  seeded, and sliced
2 to 4 Thai peppers, cut
  into ¼-inch rings
1 habañero or Scotch bonnet pepper,
  cut into ¼-inch rings (optional)
2 to 4 Chinese long peppers, cut into
  ¼-inch rings

1 poblano pepper, stemmed,
  seeded, and sliced
½ red bell pepper, stemmed,
  seeded, and sliced
½ yellow bell pepper, stemmed,
  seeded, and sliced
½ orange bell pepper, stemmed,
  seeded, and sliced
1 Anaheim pepper, stemmed,
  seeded, and sliced
8 cups clarified chicken or
  vegetable stock (page 37)
¼ head red cabbage, cut into
  wide strips
Rice or bread, for serving

1. Preheat the oven to 450°F. Coat a roasting pan with peanut oil.

2. Dredge the pork in flour. Shake off any excess flour and put in the roasting pan. Roast for 15 minutes, turn the pork over, and roast for another 10 minutes, or until the pork is browned. Add 1 cup of water and cover the pan with a lid or aluminum foil. Cook for 30 to 45 minutes, or until the pork is very tender and can easily be pulled apart with a fork. Set aside.

3. Pour the sesame oil into a soup pot over high heat. Add the garlic and stir it quickly to coat with the oil. When the garlic begins to turn golden, add the onion. Stir again to coat with oil. Reduce the temperature to medium-high, cover the pot, and allow the onion to sauté until tender. Add all the peppers, stir well to coat with oil, cover, and allow the peppers to soften.

4. Once they have grown slightly soft, add in the stock and cabbage. Stir well, cover, and reduce the heat to medium-low. Allow the soup to come to a simmer. Cook for another 10 minutes—the cabbage should be soft but still have some crunch.

5. Once the pork is cool enough to handle, pull it apart into shredded pieces. Do not worry too much about size of the shreds. Most of it will break apart once it goes into the soup. Add the shredded pork and its braising water to the soup. Stir well to incorporate all the ingredients. Remove from the heat and serve with rice or bread.

MUSHROOM MOLE
45 MINUTES PREP TIME • YIELDS TWELVE TO SIXTEEN 1-CUP SERVINGS

When I first made this soup, I used assorted mushrooms; however, I soon found out that the strong flavors of the mushrooms and the strong flavors of the mole seemed to cancel each other out. I stick with the simpler mushrooms: cremini and white button.

1 pound red new potatoes, washed and diced
6 tablespoons olive oil
1 yellow onion, sliced
2 pounds white button and cremini mushrooms, stemmed, caps wiped
clean, and cut into ⅛-inch slices
1 teaspoon kosher salt
3 cups mole sauce (page 170)
6 cups Basic Vegetable Stock (page 31)
Bread, for serving

1. Preheat the oven to 450°F. Toss the potatoes in 2 tablespoons of the olive oil in a roasting pan. Roast for 20 minutes, or until the potatoes are tender, the skin shrivels, and the flesh begins to turn a golden brown. Stir the potatoes every 10 minutes to keep them from burning. Set aside.

2. Heat the remaining 4 tablespoons of olive oil in a soup pot over high heat. Add the onion. Stir well to coat with the oil, cover the pot, and allow the onion to sauté until tender and slightly translucent. Add the mushrooms. Stir well again, cover, and sauté until the mushrooms reduce in volume and are tender. If you want to help extract some of their water quickly, add the salt to the pot when you add the mushrooms. Once the mushrooms are tender, add the potatoes, mole sauce, and stock. Cover, reduce the heat to medium, and allow the soup to reach a simmer. Serve with bread. Make sure to warn your guests that this is a hot and spicy soup!

SALADS AND MORE

SOUTHERN-STYLE BAKED MACARONI AND CHEESE

1½ HOURS PREP TIME • SERVES 16 PEOPLE

You will be very happy I included this recipe. This macaroni and cheese recipe is the most obscenely rich and decadent version I have ever run across. Remember it is a Southern recipe, so of course it isn't supposed to be good for you! It is the definition of comfort food.

- 2 cups milk, or more if needed
- 1 pound Velveeta cheese, cubed
- 4 ounces smoked Gouda cheese, grated
- 4 ounces Muenster cheese, grated
- 4 ounces cream cheese, cubed
- 4 ounces smoked white cheddar, grated
- ¼ cup unsalted butter
- ½ nutmeg, grated
- 2 teaspoons cracked black peppercorns
- ½ teaspoon cayenne
- 2 tablespoons Dijon mustard
- 2 tablespoons Worcestershire sauce
- 4 tablespoons kosher salt
- 2 pounds shell pasta
- 2 eggs

1. Preheat the oven to 350°F. Heavily grease a 9- x 13-inch pan and set aside.

2. Combine the milk, all the cheeses, and butter in a soup pot over medium heat. Cook until all the lumps of cheese have melted. Pour the mixture out of the pot and into a bowl that will hold it all. Clean out the pot.

3. Add the nutmeg, peppercorns, cayenne, mustard, and Worcestershire sauce to the cheese mixture. Whisk them in so that everything is evenly distributed. If the mixture is really thick, add another cup of milk to thin it out a bit.

4. Pour 4 quarts of water and the kosher salt into the clean soup pot. Cover and set the pot over high heat and allow it to come to a boil. Add the pasta to the water. Stir a couple of times to keep the pasta from sticking together. Cover the pot again and cook the pasta for 9 minutes, or until it is al dente. Pour the pasta into a colander and allow the excess water to drain from it. Do not rinse the pasta or allow it to cool.

5. Add the eggs to the melted cheese. Whisk them into the mixture.

6. Pour half of the pasta into the greased pan. Pour all of the cheese over the pasta. Add the rest of the pasta to the cheese. Gently stir the contents of the pan to evenly spread the cheese and pasta together. Be careful not to scrape off any of the oil coating the pan; this oil is the only way you will be able to get the macaroni and cheese out of the pan without much difficulty. Cover the pan with aluminum foil and place in the oven for 30 minutes. Remove the aluminum foil and bake, uncovered, for another 15 minutes.

7. Set the pan on a cooling rack and allow it to cool for at least 20 minutes before serving.

SPRING FRUIT SALAD with WASABI-LIME VINAIGRETTE
10 MINUTES PREP TIME [NOT INCLUDING DRESSING PREP] • INDIVIDUAL SERVING

I love wasabi. The heat from the dressing to this salad perfectly accompanies the sweet and tart flavors of the fresh spring fruit. I was continuously amused watching people eat this salad: loving every bite but coping with the fiery heat of the wasabi. I admit I am a little bit of a sadist when it comes to my food. In the end it really is all about challenging the customers to try something new.

> 3 leaves romaine lettuce, washed and patted dry
> 1 ring of pineapple, quartered
> 4 pieces fresh mango
> 4 thin strips fresh papaya
> Four 1-inch pieces honeydew melon
> ¼ cup diced red onion
> ¼ cucumber, peeled, seeded, and sliced
> 2 tablespoons minced jicama
> Wasabi-Lime Vinaigrette (recipe follows)
> Toasted sesame seeds, for garnish
> Bread, for serving

1. Place the romaine on a large plate and set aside.

2. Place all of the fruit, onion, cucumber, and jicama in a bowl. Add 1 to 2 tablespoons of the vinaigrette to the fruit. Stir well to evenly coat everything. Place the fruit on the romaine. Sprinkle with toasted sesame seeds and serve with bread.

S.O.U.P.S.

WASABI-LIME VINAIGRETTE
MAKES 2 CUPS

1.7-ounce container wasabi powder
¼ cup lime juice
1 cup rice wine vinegar
1 cup sesame oil

1. Place the wasabi powder in a bowl. Add 2 tablespoons of water. Mix with a fork until you have a thick paste. Let sit for 10 minutes.

2. Add the lime juice, whisking to break up any lumps of wasabi. Add the vinegar and sesame oil. Whisk and pour into a squeeze bottle or jar with a spout. Shake well before using. Store in an airtight container in the refrigerator for up to 2 weeks.

HEIRLOOM TOMATO ᴀɴᴅ FRESH MOZZARELLA SALAD WITH BASIL ᴀɴᴅ ROASTED GARLIC

10 MINUTES PREP TIME • INDIVIDUAL SERVING

We go through a lot of these salads each summer. People in Seattle really, really like heirloom tomatoes. We served them on skewers but if you aren't too worried about presentation, just toss everything together and serve in a soup bowl—this salad can get kind of wet and messy.

> 1 heirloom tomato, cored and cut into 8 pieces
> 4-ounce ball fresh mozzarella, cut into 8 pieces
> 8 basil leaves, sliced very thin
> 1 head garlic, roasted (page 19), cloves left whole but removed from their skins
> Kosher salt
> Cracked black peppercorns
> 1 tablespoon olive oil
> 1 teaspoon balsamic vinegar
> 2 slices day-old baguette, toasted well

1. In a mixing bowl combine the tomato, mozzarella, basil, 4 cloves of roasted garlic, salt, peppercorns, olive oil, and vinegar. Gently toss to coat everything with the oil and vinegar.

2. Place the toasted baguette slices at the bottom of a soup bowl and pour the salad over them. Serve immediately.

This was the first seasonal salad I created at the pub. It was enough of a success that I knew I would have to continue on the path of rotating menu options.

> **2 cups lightly packed mixed autumn greens**
> **Gorgonzola Dressing (recipe follows)**
> **Small handful pecans, halved and toasted**
> **2 tablespoons dried black currants**
> **Bread, for serving**

1. Place the mixed greens in a bowl. Add 1 to 2 tablespoons of the dressing and toss with the greens until they are evenly coated. Place the greens on a salad plate. Sprinkle with the toasted pecan halves and dried currants. Serve with bread.

GORGONZOLA DRESSING
MAKES 2½ CUPS

½ cup crumbled gorgonzola cheese
1 teaspoon kosher salt
2 teaspoons cracked black peppercorns
1 tablespoon garlic powder
2 tablespoons roasted garlic
1 cup mayonnaise
½ cup buttermilk

1. Place ¼ cup of the gorgonzola in the food processor along with the salt, pepper, garlic powder, roasted garlic, and mayonnaise. Purée to a smooth and creamy consistency. Occasionally scrape down the sides with a spatula.

2. Add the buttermilk and purée until the consistency thins out but is even in texture. Remove the dressing from the food processor and pour it into a bowl. Add the remaining ¼ cup of gorgonzola to the dressing. Stir well to separate all the lumps. Place in an airtight container and store in the refrigerator for up to 2 weeks.

MIXED AUTUMN GREENS with CREAMY MAPLE-HAZELNUT VINAIGRETTE and TOASTED HAZELNUTS, CURRANTS, PEAR, and GOAT CHEESE

5 MINUTES PREP TIME (NOT INCLUDING THE DRESSING PREP TIME) • INDIVIDUAL SERVING

This salad rocks! I don't think that there is a single thing that doesn't work in this salad. It is a perfect combination of sweet, sour, crunchy, and creamy goodness. I highly recommend serving it with the Southwestern Pumpkin Soup (page 116).

> 2 cups lightly packed mixed autumn greens
> 1 tablespoon Maple-Hazelnut Vinaigrette (recipe follows)
> 1 tablespoon crumbled soft goat cheese
> 1 tablespoon toasted and chopped hazelnuts
> 1 tablespoon dried black currants
> 4 slices ripe pear
> Bread, for serving

1. Place the greens in a bowl. Add the vinaigrette to the greens and toss until everything is evenly coated. Place the greens on a salad plate and top with the goat cheese, toasted hazelnuts, currants, and a fan of sliced pear. Serve with bread.

MAPLE-HAZELNUT VINAIGRETTE
MAKES ABOUT 2 CUPS

¾ cup pure maple syrup
1 egg yolk, or 1 tablespoon egg substitute or pasteurized egg yolks
2 tablespoons roasted garlic
1 tablespoon garlic powder
1 teaspoon kosher salt
2 teaspoons cracked black peppercorns
2 tablespoons minced fresh rosemary
2 tablespoons minced fresh thyme
2 cups hazelnut oil
¼ cup white wine vinegar

1. Place the first 8 ingredients, (everything except the oil and vinegar), in the food processor. Purée until all the ingredients are evenly mixed.

2. While the food processor is on, slowly drizzle the oil in through the feed tube. When all the oil is incorporated, add the vinegar. Allow the dressing to pale in color and thin in texture before turning off the machine. Remove the vinaigrette from the bowl and store in an air-tight container in the refrigerator for up to 1 week.

10 MINUTES PREP TIME [NOT INCLUDING DRESSING PREP] • INDIVIDUAL SERVING

This salad will always remind me of my childhood—specifically visiting my grandmother in Florida. In the winter this simple salad was often served for family dinners. It certainly helped that she had pecan trees, grapefruit trees, and avocado trees in her yard so it was an inexpensive salad to make! I was amazed at how tasty it was, so twenty-five years later I decided to try and repeat it. The customers seemed to really enjoy the tropical flavors; however, I am sure this version pales in comparison to my grandmother's own recipe, which I never got my hands on!

> **3 leaves romaine lettuce, washed, patted dry, and chopped**
> **½ avocado, sliced**
> **½ pink grapefruit, sectioned**
> **¼ cup toasted pecan halves**
> **Lemon-Thyme Vinaigrette (recipe follows)**
> **Bread and butter, for serving**

1. Place the romaine on a salad plate. Top with a fan of avocado slices and a fan of grapefruit sections. Sprinkle the toasted pecans around the salad and then drizzle with the vinaigrette. Serve with bread and butter.

LEMON-THYME VINAIGRETTE
MAKES 2 CUPS

Grated zest and juice of 1 lemon
2 tablespoons minced fresh thyme
1 tablespoon garlic powder
1 teaspoon kosher salt
2 teaspoons cracked black peppercorns
½ cup white wine vinegar
1 cup olive oil

1. Place all the ingredients, except the oil, in a food processor. Pulse until everything is evenly distributed. Occasionally scrape down the sides of the bowl.

2. With the processor running, slowly add the oil through the feed tube into the bowl. The slower you pour the more emulsified the dressing will become. When all the oil is added, pour the dressing into an air-tight container and store in the refrigerator for up to 1 week.

ENDIVE and WATERCRESS SALAD with WHITE BEANS, GORGONZOLA, and ORANGE-THYME VINAIGRETTE

10 MINUTES PREP [NOT INCLUDING DRESSING AND WHITE BEAN MIXTURE PREP] • INDIVIDUAL SERVING

This salad was something of an experiment. I wanted a hearty winter salad so I knew I wanted to use beans. Since we already use black beans at the pub I wanted to try something different. I like white beans. I knew their creamy texture went quite nicely with gorgonzola, so I figured why not! This artistic plate with the radial arrangement of the endive also serves a practical purpose—you can use the endive leaves to scoop up the salad mix.

> 14-ounce can white beans, drained and rinsed
> ½ cup crumbled gorgonzola cheese
> 1 cup walnuts, toasted and chopped
> 2 tablespoons minced fresh rosemary
> 1 teaspoon kosher salt
> 2 teaspoons cracked black peppercorns
> 4 tablespoons olive oil
> 1 bunch watercress, rinsed, patted dry, and stems removed
> 1 small head Belgian endive, leaves separated and wiped clean
> Orange-Thyme Vinaigrette (recipe follows)
> Bread, for serving

1. Place the beans in a bowl. Add the cheese, walnuts, rosemary, salt, pepper, and oil to the bowl and stir well. Place in a container and store in the refrigerator until you are ready to assemble the salad.

SALADS and MORE

2. Place a small pile of the watercress in the center of a round salad plate. Next, arrange the endive leaves around the edge of the plate like flower petals in a radial fashion. Then add a scoop of the bean mixture to the center of the plate, right on top of the watercress. Finally, shake the dressing and then drizzle it all over the entire salad. Serve with bread.

ORANGE-THYME VINAIGRETTE
MAKES 2 CUPS

Grated zest and juice of 1 orange
2 tablespoons minced fresh thyme
2 tablespoons roasted garlic
1 teaspoon kosher salt
2 teaspoons cracked black peppercorns
½ cup white wine vinegar
1 cup olive oil

1. Place all the ingredients, except the oil, in the food processor. Pulse until everything is evenly distributed. Occasionally scrape down the sides of the bowl.

2. With the processor running, slowly add the oil through the feed tube. The slower you pour the more emulsified the dressing will become. When all the oil is added turn off the processor and pour the dressing into an air-tight container. Store the dressing in the refrigerator until you are ready to make the salad or up to 1 week.

Strangely enough, some of the pub's patrons began coming in for the Hopvine's cookies. I said to myself, "They're just cookies, what's the big deal???" Well, apparently these cookies *are* a big deal. Upon watching the customers savor them, I think I figured out what it is that makes them so desirable. They have the amount of chips and nuts in them that we always wanted as kids but that our mothers were never willing to put in. My personal opinion about cookie dough is that it exists only to hold the chips and nuts together.

- 1 cup unsalted butter, at room temperature
- ¾ cup (packed) brown sugar
- ¾ cup granulated sugar
- 2 eggs
- 1 tablespoon vanilla extract
- ½ teaspoon salt
- ½ teaspoon baking soda
- 2½ cups unbleached flour
- 4 cups semisweet chocolate chips
- 4 cups hazelnuts, toasted, skins removed, and coarsely chopped

1. Preheat the oven to 375°F. Line a cookie sheet with parchment paper.

2. Place the butter, brown sugar, and granulated sugar in the mixer. Beat with whisk attachment on high speed until the mixture becomes extremely light and fluffy. Scrape the sides of the bowl occasionally to incorporate all the butter and sugar. Reduce the speed to low and add the eggs and vanilla. Once the eggs are folded into the batter, return the mixer's speed to high and let it whip for a few minutes.

3. Mix the salt, baking soda, and flour together in a separate bowl. Reduce the mixer's speed to low again and slowly add the flour in small batches. When the flour is completely incorporated into the batter, turn the mixer's speed back to high for a few seconds, just to make sure that the flour is evenly distributed within the batter. Turn off and remove the bowl from the mixer.

4. Add the chips and nuts to the batter. Stir well with a heavy wooden spoon. Make sure to stir from the bottom towards the top to get all the dough spread evenly. Portion out golf ball–size dough balls and place them on your cookie sheet. Press each dough ball down with the palm of your hand to about ½ inch thick. Make sure that there is at least 1 inch separating each cookie to leave room to spread.

5. Bake for 13 minutes, or until golden and the edges are just starting to turn brown. Remove from the oven and set the cookies on cooling racks until they are cold enough to store. Repeat with the rest of the dough until finished.

These are just evil! There are three things to know about these brownies: The chocolate you use really matters; these are fudge brownies, *not* cake brownies; they taste great with stout ale.

> 1½ pounds sweet dark chocolate
> 2 cups unsalted butter, cubed
> 8 eggs, at room temperature
> 4 cups sugar
> 2 tablespoons hot water
> 1½ cups instant coffee crystals
> 1 tablespoon vanilla extract
> 3½ cups unbleached white flour
> ½ teaspoon baking powder

1. Preheat the oven to 400°F. Thoroughly grease a 16- x 12-inch jelly-roll pan. Place a piece of parchment paper over the bottom of the pan.

2. Chop the chocolate into small pieces and place in a bowl along with the butter. Set the bowl over a pot of steaming water. Allow the chocolate and butter to melt completely. Remove from the steaming pot, set aside, and allow to cool for a few minutes.

3. Place the eggs and sugar in the mixer. Beat on medium with the whisk attachment until all the eggs are broken and all of the sugar is wet. Increase the speed to high and beat until very light and very fluffy.

4. Place the hot water into a container of with instant coffee, seal, and then shake well to dissolve all of the coffee crystals. Pour this into the sugar along with the vanilla extract. When thoroughly combined, remove the bowl from the mixer and set aside.

5. In another bowl mix the flour and the baking powder. Make sure that the baking powder is evenly distributed and that there are no lumps in the flour.

6. Pour the egg and sugar mixture into the melted chocolate. Stir well to evenly distribute everything. Scrape from the bottom of the chocolate bowl to mix the chocolate into the batter. Pour the flour into the chocolate and stir well to disperse. As soon as the flour is completely dispersed throughout, pour the batter into the prepared pan. Use a spatula to gently spread the batter into the corners.

7. Bake for about 25 minutes, or until the brownies are set but still soft. Remove the pan from the oven and allow it to cool for 1 hour. Cut the brownies into 4-inch squares. If storing until later, wrap each brownie with plastic wrap and store in an airtight container.

INDEX

ACKNOWLEDGMENTS

Special thanks to Deliverance, my greatest ally, who consistently told me that I needed to write a book and that I had it in me. Thank you from the bottom of my heart. This one is for you and Go. Buck, Louisa, and Jennifer Congdon, my first true guinea pigs. Hey, isn't that what family's for? Charlie from Cassis, who taught me the meaning of the term "raft." Cody Heyn, for the lovely picture of me wearing a datura hat. My guinea pigs: Bob Brenlin, Gregory Cox, Susan Filkins, Alex Pina, Clif Marr, Sheila Bernstein, Michal Balun, Michelle Kastor, Merlin Rainwater, Joshua Casto, Cathy Phillips, Eric Johnson, Julia Demarest, my mother, my father, Milton Roff, Kathy Bauer, and Marcus Denniston, all of whom were willing to test my soups out at their homes and give me some greatly valuable feedback. My editor Sally, to whom fate introduced me, and Bob Brenlin, without whom the ideas for this book would have never manifested. Last, but not least the Hopvine Pub and all its employees, who were willing to push my soups like dealers to unsuspecting customers.

ABOUT THE AUTHOR

CODY HEVN

When Michael Congdon was a very young boy, he announced that he wished the whole world was a chocolate chip cookie. His parents asked him what he would do with it then, and he responded that he would eat it. His father then asked him where he would stand while eating the cookie. Michael didn't answer.

As precocious as Michael was, here he is today, eating that proverbial cookie and standing on his own two feet (that's where, dad!). While this cookbook grew from Michael's simple desire to no longer write down these recipes for customers on the back of ticket paper, he is immensely pleased with the direction this book has led him. Michael's new passion is ice cream—the stranger the better. When Michael is asked if there is another book in the works, his response is, " . . . Maybe. Talk to Maxfield. He'll know more."